DOING YOUTH PARTICIPATORY ACTION RESEARCH

"Timely and compelling . . . The co-authors integrate researchers, teachers and students into a framework that will appeal broadly. YPAR is quite popular in youth studies, urban education and psychology—and there is no other volume that navigates the 'how to' with the 'theory' and the exemplars in the ways that these writers do. This is a strong moment for a volume like this, when there is much dissatisfaction with the traditional 'evidence'-based policy regime, but few alternatives."

Michelle Fine
The Graduate Center, City University
of New York, USA

Doing Youth Participatory Action Research offers an unprecedented, in-depth exploration of the pragmatics and possibilities of youth-driven research. Drawing upon multiple years of experience engaging youth in rigorous, critical inquiry about the conditions impacting their lives, the authors examine how YPAR encourages the educational community to re-imagine the capabilities of young people and the purposes of teaching, learning, and research itself.

Much more than a "how-to" guide for those interested in creating their own YPAR projects, this book draws upon the voices of students and educators, as well as the multiple historical traditions of critical research, to describe how youth inquiry transforms each step of the traditional research process. From identifying research questions to collecting data and disseminating findings, each chapter details how YPAR revolutionizes traditional conceptions of who produces knowledge, how it is produced, and for what purposes. The book weaves together research, policy, and practice to offer YPAR as a practice with the power to challenge entrenched social and educational inequalities, empower critically aware youth, and revolutionize pedagogy in classrooms and communities.

For researchers, educators, community members, and youth who want to connect, question, and transform the world collectively, *Doing Youth Participatory Action Research* is a rich source of both pragmatic methodological guidance and inspiration.

Nicole Mirra is an Assistant Professor of English Education at The University of Texas at El Paso, USA.

Antero Garcia is an Assistant Professor in the English Department at Colorado State University, USA.

Ernest Morrell is Director of the Institute for Urban and Minority Education and Professor of English Education at Teachers College, Columbia University, USA, and 2015 National Council of Teachers of English President.

Language, Culture, and Teaching
Sonia Nieto, Series Editor

Visit **www.routledge.com/education** for additional information on titles in the **Language, Culture, and Teaching** series.

DOING YOUTH PARTICIPATORY ACTION RESEARCH

Transforming Inquiry with Researchers, Educators, and Students

Nicole Mirra
Antero Garcia
Ernest Morrell

Routledge
Taylor & Francis Group

NEW YORK AND LONDON

First published 2016
by Routledge
711 Third Avenue, New York, NY 10017

and by Routledge
2 Park Square, Milton Park, Abingdon, Oxon OX14 4RN

Routledge is an imprint of the Taylor & Francis Group, an informa business

First edition published by Routledge

Library of Congress Cataloging-in-Publication Data
Mirra, Nicole.
  Doing youth participatory action research : a methodological handbook
for researchers, educators, and youth / by Nicole Mirra, Antero Garcia, and
Ernest Morrell.
    pages cm. — (Language, culture, and teaching)
  Includes bibliographical references and index.
  1. Action research in education—Handbooks, manuals, etc.   2. Education—
Research—Handbooks, manuals, etc.   I. Garcia, Antero.   II. Morrell,
Ernest, 1971–   III. Title.
   LB1028.24.M56 2016
   370.72—dc23
   2015016118

ISBN: 978-1-138-81356-4 (hbk)
ISBN: 978-1-138-81357-1 (pbk)
ISBN: 978-1-315-74804-7 (ebk)

Typeset in Bembo
by Apex CoVantage, LLC

CONTENTS

FOREWORD

Conventional wisdom would have us believe that young people, especially young people of color who live in poverty, have little to bring to their education, and even less to teach their elders. The deficit discourses surrounding these young people focus principally on what they *can't do*, *don't have*, and *can't learn*: "They don't have books at home," "They don't have fathers," "They can't speak English," or "They can't do demanding work until they learn 'the basics'" are typical comments. These and other such ideas fill media accounts about public education, even making their way into teachers' rooms. The bottom line: poor students of color are "different" (read, not quite as worthy, or as intelligent) from majority-group White, English-speaking, and middle-class students. The solution? To "fix" them with regimented learning, scripted curricula, high-stakes tests, and uninspired pedagogy.

Youth participatory action research (YPAR) is a welcome antidote to these tired policies and practices. In this book, authors Nicole Mirra, Antero Garcia, and Ernest Morrell not only challenge such ideas, but they also make the case that it is *precisely* young people like these who have much to teach teachers, teacher educators, and policymakers about what matters in education. Based on fifteen years of collaboration, the book chronicles one year of the UCLA Council of Youth Research, a group of high school students, graduate students, classroom teachers, and university professors engaged in cutting-edge YPAR. Throughout the text, the authors ask us to consider what public schooling can become if it takes seriously the mission of public schools to provide all children with a high quality education.

Doing Youth Participatory Action Research demonstrates unequivocally that young people, particularly those who have been denied an affirming and high quality education, can understand and benefit from intellectually challenging and complex texts. Reading this book, you will be forced to rethink old ideas about who can do research, and how. The young researchers, using a range of methodologies, uncover truths that may elude even more seasoned scholars, in the process pointing the way to education that is both more caring and more demanding. With a compelling mix of theory, method, stories, and insightful interludes, the researchers—from high school students to veteran professors—paint a picture of engaged, enthusiastic participants co-creating spaces of hope and empowerment.

Although there are a growing number of books about YPAR, relatively little is available about how to do it. What is especially unique about this volume is that it successfully connects the *how* with the *what* and *why* of participatory action research. Part guide, part story, part inspirational testimony about what can happen when teachers believe in the capacity of their students to think creatively and to change their ideas and practices accordingly, it is a moving narrative of collaborative work whose purpose is to make meaningful change. YPAR can become, as the authors point out, a life-changing experience for all participants.

Questions need to be asked about any research, and some of these include: Who tells the stories? How are they told? Who has the right to speak for the silenced? Who benefits from the stories that are told? In this sense, important questions about the nature of research, and whether it can ever be truly objective, are also broached. Despite protestations from some in the academy that research must always be neutral, objective, "scientific," and therefore not to be sullied by human lives and concerns, in the end, all research is about telling stories. Once this reality is accepted, perhaps the most we can expect is that it be fair and just, and that is exactly what we see in these pages.

Doing Participatory Action Research is a particularly welcome addition to the Language, Culture, and Teaching Series. With its focus on creative and empowering approaches to language and literacy, the series includes books on critical pedagogy, family engagement, bilingualism and biculturalism, diversity of all kinds, and social justice broadly understood. YPAR fits in well with these issues, and it broadens the series parameters to include penetrating questions about humanizing curriculum and pedagogy, as well as about research and representation.

"This work is morally important," the authors of this inspiring book point out in the final chapter. They demonstrate how the YPAR process itself helped them become better human beings, more caring teachers, and even better researchers. The ethical dimension of teaching, learning, and researching has too often unfortunately been missing in discussions of public education. In contrast, in these pages, relationship building is presented as a pedagogical strategy, not simply as a "feel-good" way to make schools more palatable to students who have been turned off by too many years of indifferent, cold, and callous schooling. *Doing Youth Participatory Action Research* reminds us that words such as caring, love, and solidarity need to be part and parcel of what education is about.

Sonia Nieto

PREFACE

Over the past fifteen years, the three of us have been working with generations of public high school students from South and East Los Angeles who develop, conduct, and share original research about educational and social issues that deeply and directly impact their lives through a process called Youth Participatory Action Research (YPAR). The topics they have taken up, among many others, include hot button educational issues such as the impact of the nationwide economic crisis on public education, the controversy over zero tolerance discipline policies, and the proliferation of charter schools in urban school districts. These young people, drawn from struggling schools and communities by caring teachers who recognized their potential, have presented their research, in the form of multimedia presentations replete with sophisticated survey and interview data, to audiences ranging from teachers to community leaders to educational researchers in locations as diverse as Los Angeles City Hall, school cafeterias, labor centers, and national academic conferences.

Each time the young people share their research, educators and researchers surround them (and us), eager to ask, "How did you learn to do this work?" and "How can I bring YPAR back to my students?" We've met so many educators over the years who are searching for ways to engage students in learning that prepares them for college and career in ways that are meaningful, socially aware, and embedded in the unique contexts in which they live. We wrote this book as a labor of love to share the practices of our Council family and inspire others to cultivate and amplify the voices of the young people in their lives.

Over our years of writing academic publications and giving conference presentations about this work, we have also realized that YPAR offers unique methodological and analytical insights to the landscape of educational research. Our book seeks to synthesize the theory, history, and process of YPAR into a guide that will be accessible to both researchers and practitioners and provide the information needed to make this civically engaging and justice motivated practice more commonly practiced in schools, communities, and the academy.

In this book we offer the story of the Council as a case study through which to analyze the workings of YPAR amidst the deeper context of public education today. We demonstrate how critical research opens up possibilities for new innovations that continue to honor the curiosity, hope, and potential of young people. This has been an exhilarating professional journey for us, but much more importantly, a deeply personal one as well. Working with the Council has been among the most rewarding and meaningful experiences in our lives; it has influenced our trajectories as academics and pushed us to become better human beings to live up to the trust and faith that our amazing group of young people have placed in us.

Our goal is that this book, with its multiplicity of voices but clear focus on the theory and process of YPAR, demystifies the potential and possibilities of youth-driven research and demonstrates the wonders that emerge when we expect great things from young people. We hope that you fall in love with the Council community just as we have and use the inspiration to develop a new wave of transformative educational and research methodologies.

Overview of the Book

We begin by explaining how urgently needed YPAR is in an educational context riven by inequality and standardization. We detail the ways that YPAR challenges traditional ideas about who conducts research, how research is conducted, and for what purposes in ways that have the potential to humanize and empower youth, teachers, and researchers. We then introduce the Council community and describe the context of the 2010–2011 school year that we will explore through the rest of the book. Before delving into the Council's story, our second chapter deconstructs each term that comprises the YPAR acronym, asking in turn about the theories that have historically defined research, action, participation, and youth in order to set the stage for an in-depth exploration of the YPAR process.

The following chapters lead the reader through the research cycle through the eyes of the Council members and detail the unique contributions that YPAR has made to re-conceptualizing each step in the process, from identifying problems and developing research questions to collecting and analyzing data to disseminating findings. Each chapter features the voices of young people and educators engaged in this work, providing real-world examples of how the Council tackled each step in the research process in unique ways. We also include short interludes couched between the chapters that give Council members opportunities to talk about the impact of YPAR on their personal, academic, and professional lives in their own words. After telling the Council's story, we offer some guidance about the tensions and possibilities of pursuing YPAR as professional practice within university settings. We conclude with a call to action for all members of the educational community to look for ways to humanize and empower young people and offer our final thoughts about sustaining the YPAR movement.

Acknowledgements

Of course, we acknowledge all of the students who have participated in the Council community over the past 15 years. They have inspired the words on these pages through their passion, intellect, dedication, and love, and we are indebted to them for bringing laughter, joy, and purpose to our work. We would also like to thank all of the teachers and graduate students who invested so much in this community over the years—your commitment to excellence and social justice propelled us through the journey of completing this book. We are grateful to our colleagues at UCLA and at our current academic institutions for supporting this work, especially to John Rogers and Jeannie Oakes from the Institute for Democracy, Education, and Access (IDEA) at UCLA, where the Council was born. We never could have taken on this work without the support of the UCLA IDEA team from that year: Jerchel Anderson, Claudia Bustamante, Carolyn Castelli, Jessie Castro, Nery Orellana, and Jared Planas. Thanks to Naomi Silverman and Sonia Nieto, our editors, for believing in the power of our story and being patient with us as it took shape. And to our families, an extra special thank you for sharing us with the Council family and sustaining us as we do what we love.

1

INTRODUCTION

Close your eyes and recall the most meaningful and rewarding learning experiences of your life. What were the characteristics that those experiences had in common? They likely built upon your personal interests and connected you to a wider community of fellow learners. They probably broadened your horizons and introduced you to people and ideas that you had not previously encountered. And they hopefully transformed you personally or professionally and propelled you on to joyous lifelong journeys of exploration.

This is the kind of learning that not only alters what individuals know and can do, but who they are. It can (and does) change lives. It is the kind of learning that parents desperately desire for their children and that educators strive to provide to their students.

The three of us wrote this book because we have been privileged enough to experience this kind of learning ourselves. The particular learning experience that we document here involves the work we have done over the past fifteen years with hundreds of young people in Los Angeles through a program that offers literacy enrichment, civic engagement, college access, and so much more through the practice of conducting research. While its moniker has evolved since its beginnings in 1999, the program has come to be known as the UCLA Council of Youth Research—or, as we refer to it, simply the Council.

Even though programs like the Council are grounded in theories and social movements that reach back centuries, they have recently inspired the creation of new terminology in the educational research community. Youth Participatory Action Research (YPAR) is a term that gained widespread attention through Julio Cammarota and Michelle Fine's groundbreaking 2008 book *Revolutionizing Education,* which highlighted the potential of youth research to transform teaching, learning, and academic scholarship. At its most basic level, YPAR refers to the practice of mentoring young people to become social scientists by engaging them in all aspects of the research cycle, from developing research questions and examining relevant literature to collecting and analyzing data and offering findings about social issues that they find meaningful and relevant.

And yet YPAR is about so much more than simply training young people to mimic the behaviors of adult researchers. Throughout this book, we will discuss how this practice has implications for re-imagining the nature of teaching and learning in formal and informal educational spaces, the ways that education policymakers conceptualize the capabilities and aspirations of young people, and the purpose and ethics of the educational research community as a whole.

We feel that this is an important moment for the educational community to consider YPAR, for while it is generating interest and excitement among educators and researchers, much confusion remains about what it is and how it is done. Is YPAR a theory? A methodology? Simply a framework for engaging young people in research? Educators are engaging in YPAR with students of varying ages, backgrounds, and interests around the country, but for the most part these projects remain isolated and disconnected from each other and from mainstream education research, policy, and practice. We share the story of the UCLA Council of Youth Research in these pages in order to begin to develop some common language around the purpose and practice of YPAR and tease out the lessons that YPAR offers for revolutionizing public education so that all young people experience transformative learning that changes their lives and opens doors of personal, academic, and civic opportunity.

Why YPAR Now?

There are thirty-five of us huddled in a corner of the Sheraton in New Orleans, away from the presentation rooms, trying to find a quiet place in the half hour or so we have before we present. The high school students pose for pictures with their peers and their teachers. Dressed up in suits, they look like they're headed to work or church; instead, these high school students are about to deliver a presentation to the American Educational Research Association articulating the research on civic engagement and urban educational reform that they have been conducting for an entire school year.

I can sense the combination of nervousness and excitement in their voices, in their movements, as they fumble through their note cards, mouths mumbling the words they will pronounce to a crowd of educational scholars soon enough. I too think about what I want to say—but not to the audience. My concern are these twenty-five 15- to 17-year-olds, my graduate students who work with the project, and the teachers who have all made this nearly 2,000-mile trek from sunny Southern California to The Big Easy. What will we draw upon as our motivation?

Ten minutes prior to show time we convene in our usual circle. Stragglers amble out of bathrooms tucking in shirts and checking their hair. The seniors step up for our traditional pep talk and offer their words of advice and encouragement. Their use of the collective pronoun reminds me again of what we are capable of creating as a society if we only had the will, if we only paid attention, and if we only fully believed in the humanity of these students and the neighborhoods and families from which they came. Everybody wants to feel a part of something special; everyone wants to contribute. We are dreamers all, unless, of course, those dreams through time and heartache have been deferred or extinguished altogether.

But something right has happened with this Council of Youth Research. Again, 100% of the seniors are graduating and heading off to postsecondary education. They are poised, righteously indignant. They are confident, prepared—they are a team. And they are ready, once again, to share a powerful message with the world about the fallacy of equitable schooling and about the role of youth in making the world right. As always on these occasions I am overcome, more by anger than pride. I am angry because we have failed to institutionalize excellence and these moments are the exception rather than the rule. We know how to educate. We know what students need. We know what they are capable of, and the greatest tragedy of all is that we fail to do these things and we live daily with the results. As do all of the countless youth in Los Angeles and cities beyond who have no Council of Youth Research.

Ernest's reflection—his frustration, his anger—vividly illustrates the challenges characterizing today's social and educational context. We live in a polarized country in which it is becoming more and more difficult to communicate and find common ground across lines of difference created by racial, socioeconomic, and political inequalities. Communities of extreme wealth sit mere miles away from neighborhoods of extreme poverty and the academic and civic trajectories of young people correspond more to the circumstances of their birth than their aspirations and ability.

The Council students traveled to New Orleans with us to stand before educational researchers and policymakers and put a human face to the educational crises those adults studied in theory—those familiar crises of racial and civic achievement gaps, of funding inequalities, of resource shortages. Through YPAR, the students capitalized on the innate curiosity that teenagers possess about the world around them and their place within it to show these adults what they had found through their own inquiry—that some students in their city were provided with high-quality educational resources to which they themselves were not given equal access. They shared their experiences and dreams and findings, and after these adults were dazzled by their brilliance and floored by the rigor and passion of their research, the students asked of the room: *don't we deserve the resources we need to succeed, too?* They shook the moral conscience of every adult in attendance.

YPAR is crucial at this moment because it asks—or rather, demands—that we reconsider the why, how, and who of educational practice and research. Let's begin with the why—the purpose behind the choices we make in public education. Debates about educational standards and new standardized assessments revolve around the idea that the purpose of K–12 schooling is to provide students with the knowledge, skills, and competencies for college and career readiness, while the purpose of K–12 research is to document successes and failures in achieving that readiness among various subgroups of students. These goals, while certainly worthy, ignore the civic purpose of public education and the idea that schools have a role in preparing young people to become citizens and contribute to the creation of an ever more just democratic society.

By asking young people to put academic skills to use in the purpose of researching and addressing real social problems instead of engaging in hypothetical or abstract academic exercises, YPAR offers a different purpose for teaching and learning—one rooted in social change and the realization of students' capacities in all areas of life, not only those related to their economic success. And as a research paradigm, YPAR reminds adult educational researchers that inquiry about the world has a responsibility to offer that world information that can lead to the betterment of people's lives, rather than merely the advancement of one's career.

Next, the how—what qualifies as legitimate methods of educational practice and research? While critical pedagogy and critical literacy have a foothold in some classrooms today, giving some students opportunities to use their literacy skills for authentic purposes and take on identities as experts, much classroom practice remains teacher-centered and focused upon the acquisition of standardized bodies of knowledge that can be assessed through standardized tests. Similarly, the educational policy community continues to value large-scale quantitative studies that attempt to numerically capture and express human experience while minimizing qualitative research aimed at illuminating the factors that contribute to educational outcomes.

YPAR asks, why can't personal experience be valued as a valid form of data? Or the oral histories passed down through generations in a community? YPAR encourages young people to explode traditional ideas of knowledge production and use forms of creative expression to share what they know. YPAR also debunks the notion that adult researchers cannot create bonds with participants in their research or take personal part in the research process itself. It encourages us to reconsider how we know what we know and what might be the best methods with which to express that knowledge.

Finally, the who—who is permitted to create knowledge in our society? Whose voices possess legitimacy? The educational establishment, with few exceptions, treats young people as objects rather than subjects throughout their academic trajectories. Adults debate among themselves about what students need and then implement the initiatives that they agree are in students' best interests. Young people rarely have the opportunity to provide their insights into how and for what purposes they want to be educated; and indeed, on the rare occasions their input is solicited, youth don't always know what to say because they have never been afforded chances to engage in this kind of thought.

The most revolutionary aspect of YPAR is the realization of the full humanity of young people. YPAR demands that we embrace the potential in all students by offering them opportunities to name, explore, and analyze their experiences, and respect them as authors and experts of their own lives. It also demands humility of adult researchers, reminding them of their duty to honor those who entrust them with their stories and to strive to share in the struggle toward social justice.

Our understanding of the power of YPAR has developed over time through our labor of love with the Council, and it is with the benefit of over 15 years of exploration that we now turn back to analyze how the Council began and choose a slice of the work to focus on in this book.

Origins of the UCLA Council of Youth Research

The work of the Council began in 1997, though at that time it was known as the Futures Project and operated at only one Los Angeles area high school. Through a partnership with the Santa Monica–Malibu Unified School District and the Annenberg Foundation, UCLA professors Jeannie Oakes and John Rogers collaborated with Santa Monica High School to address persistent race and class inequalities in academic achievement.

During their discussions, John developed the core idea that would guide what eventually became the Council: that students should be welcomed into the conversations about the academic pathways offered at their school considering their firsthand experience in the classrooms and other learning spaces on campus. John and his team began working with students in a 9th grade college support class to study academic opportunities by having the freshmen interview seniors about their high school experiences—an endeavor that continued into their sophomore year.

At the end of that year, in the summer of 1999, the team sponsored the first summer seminar on the UCLA campus in order to give these Futures students research training so that they could continue to work proactively to address challenges in their school. By this time, Ernest had joined the UCLA team and taken a leadership role in the program. The summer seminar was so powerful for all involved that Ernest began brainstorming ways to open up the opportunity to more students from different schools across Los Angeles with a particular focus on low-income students of color who attended some of the city's most troubled, high-poverty schools and could benefit dramatically personally and academically from this empowering learning space.

As the Democratic National Convention prepared to descend upon Los Angeles in August 2000, the summer seminar expanded to offer students from across the city the opportunity to contribute their voices and ideas about the directions in which they thought the country should be headed. In the years to follow, the Futures program morphed into the Council of Youth Research and engaged student teams from five schools across the city in developing critical research skills, analyzing the major tenets of critical sociology, and sharing their projects in culminating presentations to adult policymakers, educators, and community leaders.

The topics that Council students explored evolved over the years in response to major current events; for example, students interviewed civil rights leaders and conducted original historical research about diversity and access in Los Angeles in 2004 to commemorate the 50th anniversary of the *Brown v. Board of Education* Supreme Court decision. They explored the impacts of the budget cuts on Los Angeles schools in 2009 as California reeled from the effects of the national economic recession. In all cases, however, these events provided merely a frame within which students developed and explored research questions that they found meaningful. They worked in teams supported by teachers and UCLA researchers to develop their multimedia projects.

By the time that Nicole and Antero began their studies in the Urban Schooling doctoral program at UCLA in 2008 and learned about the Council from John and Ernest (their advisors), the program had gained enough financial backing to support the hiring of a program coordinator as well as several graduate student researchers. Nicole, Antero, and a team of fellow doctoral students began working with Council students and their guiding teachers year-round as the summer seminar segued into weekly after-school meetings, Saturday seminars, and springtime presentations. The Council had solidified its reputation as a program that offered young people who attended struggling schools in South and East Los Angeles the opportunity to see themselves as knowledge producers and explore the challenges facing their communities through the research process.

Focus of This Book: Case Study of the 2010–2011 School Year

While we could have filled volumes exploring the work of the Council over the past (nearly) two decades, we believe that providing a detailed story of the Council at a particular moment in time offers readers an in-depth portrait that is both specific to one year but also generalizable enough to resonate in a variety of current educational contexts as well. The 2010–2011 school year represented a high point in our ability to actualize our YPAR model to its fullest potential for several reasons.

First, we were enjoying the financial support of multiple foundations, as well as the City of Los Angeles, which enabled us to provide stipends to teachers and graduate students, give summer jobs to our young participants, offer technology and other learning resources to support student research, and travel to research sites and professional conferences to share findings. This represented a level of support that was unusual not only for our group, but for almost all of the YPAR projects with which we are familiar. While it may seem impractical to lay out a vision for this work based on such a rare, highly resourced example, we feel that the impact that the year's activities had on students and teachers justifies telling the story, showing what is possible, and asking what resources we are willing to commit to creating transformative educational opportunities for all young people.

Second, we had reached a point at which the collective knowledge, experience, and commitment of the educators involved in implementing the program had created a sort of YPAR dream team. Ernest and John had over a decade of experience under their belts from which to draw as they designed the yearly plan; Nicole had hit her stride in coordinating the logistics for the program; and she, Antero, and the rest of the graduate students and teachers had built relationships based on previous work together that set the stage for a powerful and collaborative experience. Again, we focus on this year not only to celebrate the accomplishments of an extraordinary group of individuals, but to document the time and effort needed to build this kind of critical community among adults and young people.

Finally, we decided to focus on the 2010–2011 school year in this book because it was during this year that we dedicated our work to the exploration of issues that continue to resonate in today's educational context—the educational opportunities to which all young people are entitled and the race- and class-based inequalities surrounding who actually receives those opportunities.

In the spring of 2010, when planning began for a new cycle of Council research set to begin that summer, Ernest and John could not shake a particular (and not particularly happy) anniversary from their minds. California was marking the tenth anniversary of the filing of the *Williams v. California* superior court case. The lawsuit, filed on behalf of nearly 100 low-income students of color attending segregated schools in San Francisco County, contended that the state failed in its responsibility to provide all students with equal access to educational resources, ranging from qualified teachers to instructional materials to adequate building facilities. UCLA's Graduate School of Education was involved in collecting and sharing data in support of the plaintiffs.

When the case was settled in 2004, the state was ordered to provide additional funding to struggling schools for resources. In spirit, the plaintiffs had won and proven that students in low-income communities of color were not receiving an equitable education. But in reality, Ernest and John knew that the schools they worked with in Los Angeles in 2010 were still suffering from a lack of resources, and that their students were still not getting what they deserved.

Court battles related to the adequacy of educational resources and the lack of equitable distribution of these resources have been waged across the country, making this a continuous hot button issue (see Michael Rebell's 2009 book, *Courts and Kids: Pursuing Educational Equity through the State Courts*, for summaries and analyses of these cases). In many of these cases, including the *Williams* case, stories are told about the experiences of individual students in order to put a face to the effects of educational inequities; however, adults are the ones who tell these stories and adults are the ones who debate among themselves about the learning resources that students need.

Ernest and John wondered: what would the students in the Council have to say about the state of public education ten years after *Williams*? What would they want to tell politicians, policymakers, educators, and their communities about their schools and what they needed from them in order to succeed? The more they thought about it, the more they realized that student voice was sorely needed to define what quality education meant in the 21st century. And so they offered the frame "The State of Education 10 Years After *Williams*" as an organizing theme for the 2010–2011 school year.

We encourage readers to think about this frame relative to the education battles raging in their own contexts and consider the extent to which the voices and experiences of young people have been honored during these conversations. Through the Council's story, we offer YPAR as a crucial practice with the potential to recast what truly matters in public education from the perspective of the students sitting in classrooms across the country.

Introducing Sites and Participants

The students who joined the Council during the summer seminar of 2010 began their YPAR journey in a well-resourced classroom at the UCLA Law School. UCLA represents a crucial site of teaching, learning, and research in this book as the academic home of the program—the site of the intellectual discussions that informed the theory and practice of the Council, as well as the home base to which students traveled each day to plan their research excursions into the greater Los Angeles metropolitan area. As we will discuss in more depth later in the book, situating the Council's work at a university setting was crucial, not only for legitimizing YPAR as serious academic work, but also for fostering a college-going culture among the Council students. As students made their way to UCLA each day of the summer seminar, we wanted them to see themselves as future college students taking ownership of the campus.

Equally important as UCLA and the city of Los Angeles as sites of study in this book were the schools that the 2010–2011 Council students attended during the school year. Students' knowledge and opinions of the public education system were forged by their experiences in these schools, and these are the schools to which students would return in order to gather most of their data from administrators, teachers, and classmates.

In keeping with the emancipatory, critical purposes espoused by the Council, the students targeted for inclusion in the program attended schools in traditionally underserved areas of Los Angeles—in this case, East Los Angeles, South Los

Angeles, and Watts. Student teams came from five high schools, each led by an educator from the community.

The East Los Angeles schools, Woodrow Wilson High School and Theodore Roosevelt High School, served mainly low-income Latina/o students, including substantial numbers of English Language Learners. The South Los Angeles and Watts schools, Crenshaw High School, Manual Arts High School, and Locke High School, served a mix of low-income African-American and Latina/o students. In keeping with trends in urban schooling across the country, these schools existed in near-constant states of turmoil as various reform efforts were adopted and disbanded in desperate efforts to raise low test scores and increase abysmal graduation rates.

For instance, Manual Arts experienced rapid turnover of principals, with new faces appearing on campus nearly every year. Roosevelt adopted different bell schedules from year to year and vacillated between comprehensive school and small learning academy models. Crenshaw and Wilson carried on under constant threat of district takeover and reconstitution, while Locke was handed over to the Green Dot charter management organization as the charter movement grew in strength across Los Angeles.

Despite these struggles, these schools also served as crucial shared institutions within communities with rich histories of protest aimed at challenging racial and educational inequity. Memories of the Watts Rebellion of 1965 and the Chicano Blowouts of 1968 persisted in public memory, and community groups like Inner City Struggle and the Community Coalition enjoyed strong track records of engaging young people in community organizing efforts. In all, this constellation of schools presented a unique and powerful context within which to pursue YPAR projects with the goal of empowering low-income students of color.

Readers will become familiar with a cast of characters from the Council community throughout this book—students, teachers, and graduate students—and some brief introductions are in order. The core group of teachers who led the Council student groups during the 2010–2011 school year included Maria Martinez (Wilson High School), Eddie Lopez (Roosevelt High School), Fred David (Crenshaw High School), Katie Rainge-Briggs (Manual Arts High School), and Laurence Tan (122nd Street Elementary School/Locke High School). Colleagues stepped in along the way when circumstances prevented folks from participating in certain events in order to offer continuous support, including Veronica Garcia Garza (Wilson High School) and Nikhil Laud (Grover Cleveland High School).

Each brought years of experience within the Los Angeles Unified School District to the Council, as well as passion for critical pedagogy and absolute dedication to the success of their students. In addition to being referenced in each chapter, these teachers will share their perspectives about the Council in their own words through short vignettes scattered throughout the book. These vignettes will illustrate the unique strengths and styles that each teacher brought to this work to build the Council family.

This family also featured a group of UCLA graduate students who supported the students and teachers in their research. In addition to Nicole and Antero, these students included: Mark Bautista, Melanie Bertrand, Ebony Cain, Arlene Ford, Monique Lane, Antonio Martinez, and D'Artagnan Scorza. Several vignettes will highlight the unique perspectives that these then-students, now-Ph.Ds. had as they participated in the Council while working on their doctorates in Urban Schooling.

Structure and Outline of the Book

While this book focuses on telling the story of the Council—one YPAR program among many—our goal in delving into our particular experiences is not to prescribe one way of approaching youth research, but to use grounded theory to uncover and share the bedrock principles and values that anyone interested in doing YPAR will find relevant and useful. We have not set out to write a "how-to" manual about doing YPAR because, as we will explore throughout the book, context is crucial and every program must build upon its own unique strengths. We simply hope that our story can be illuminating and inspiring as the YPAR movement grows.

Before we share the Council's story, we find it crucial to situate YPAR within theories and social movements that reach back centuries and emerged simultaneously in different locations around the world in order to understand the foundation upon which we stand as contemporary researchers. Chapter 2 grounds our work in extensive analysis of the theoretical and epistemological foundations of YPAR, beginning with the ideas of Greek philosophers and proceeding through to present-day critical theory and educational research. We deconstruct the concepts of youth, participation, action, and research in philosophy and practice and examine the various traditions of critical participatory action research that developed in Latin America, England, and the United States in the 19th and 20th centuries.

Chapters 3 through 7 take the reader through the major steps in the research process through the eyes of Council participants. Chapter 3 focuses on relationship-building as the primary pedagogy that drives YPAR and allows for the dismantling of the hierarchy between adults and students in pursuit of collaborative learning. We explore how unpacking and reinventing traditional power dynamics creates new opportunities to engage youth in dialogue around issues that really matter to them. We break down strategies for supporting the relational components and emotional hurdles of YPAR.

Chapter 4 explores what it means to build beyond a "problem" and how to construct critical research questions. In particular we investigate what it means to change a student's mindset from experiencing inequity to asking researchable questions about it. This process includes grounding research in literature and providing context for the injustices that students experience in their communities. We argue in this chapter that part of grounding youth in research is allowing them to see a long history of critical research and then helping them to see themselves as qualified to continue this critical conversation.

We begin Chapter 5 by offering an anecdote that reminds researchers that YPAR is not simply "kids doing what researchers do." Instead, this chapter highlights how YPAR methodology expands and extends what we count as research and how we have empirically evaluated it. We highlight how young people have a unique and powerful position as researchers and how their life experiences count as methodology. We examine how the range of YPAR methods is much wider than what tends to "count" in traditional research.

Chapter 6 looks at differences in collecting data in both in-school and out-of-school spaces. In both contexts there are various forms of insider knowledge that youth are privy to. Part of YPAR is unpacking and revealing the implicit and "obvious" aspects of school equity to explore. We reinforce in this chapter that this process is not about simply letting students conduct research amuck, but is instead a "with" process in which adult researchers engage in data collection and analysis alongside their youth peers.

In Chapter 7, we focus on the opportunities that students have to share their research findings with different audiences and how they continue the work after the presentations have ended. In particular, we focus on bringing research data back to communities, both local and academic. Further, we explore the process of connecting with policy makers and continuing the next steps of activism through the cycle of reflection and action.

Finally, we take a step back from the daily workings of the Council in Chapter 8 in order to discuss the benefits and challenges of developing YPAR initiatives while managing university faculty and research positions. In addition to exploring the tension between implementing a YPAR program and studying and publishing about it, we examine the tenuous position of YPAR as a valued methodology within the academy and share how various scholars position their work in order to simultaneously succeed within and challenge dominant research paradigms.

Interspersed between the chapters the readers will find six short vignettes that we call "interludes" offering first-person testimonials from a variety of Council participants. These interludes illuminate the theories and concepts explored in each chapter and highlight the impacts that YPAR had on the personal, professional, and civic lives of everyone in the Council family.

The first interlude offers a dialogue between Council founders Ernest Morrell and John Rogers that mines the theoretical and practical origins of the Council. The second includes a conversation between then–graduate students Mark Bautista, Ebony Cain, and Antonio Martinez about the intellectual and practical support that they offered to Council teams and the impact that the

Council had on their academic trajectories. The third features Council teachers Fred David, Veronica Garcia Garza, and Eduardo Lopez, who discuss the pedagogical strategies they employed with their students during the YPAR process.

Nicole engages in dialogue with Council teacher Katie Rainge-Briggs during the fourth interlude to explore the philosophy of love and caring that suffused the Council community. In the fifth interlude, we catch up with Council students from 2010–2011 who worked with teacher Laurence Tan at Locke High School to research leadership in order to explore how the Council influenced their personal, academic, and civic lives. Finally, the sixth interlude presents the transcript of the speech that Ernest gave at the conclusion of the Council students' presentation at the 2011 Annual Meeting of the American Educational Research Association in order to spur the educational community to action to offer transformative learning opportunities to all students.

We conclude the book by imagining how YPAR can transform the future of educational practice, policy, and research in ways that honor the voices, experiences, and literacy practices that young people from low-income communities of color bring to public life. We offer a call to action to educators to redefine their relationships to their students, their profession, and the future of public education in ways that promote justice and hope.

Reference

Rebell, M. (2009). *Courts and kids: Pursuing educational equity through the state courts.* Chicago: University of Chicago Press.

2

THE THEORETICAL AND EPISTEMOLOGICAL FOUNDATIONS OF YPAR

"You could bring in an adult to do a two-day evaluation of a school and come up with some conclusion. But if you [consult] a student who actually attends the school, that student deals with the school every day, so he or she is an expert at knowing what their peers need."

Dimitri, 12th grader

"It's important to do research [on our own] so it's not only other people who are telling our story. We are the ones living through this current education crisis."

Evelyn, 12th grader

Dimitri and Evelyn express perspectives on research that highlight the importance of enlisting those most impacted by social problems in acquiring and sharing the knowledge needed to develop possible solutions. Their sentiments differ drastically from the way these Los Angeles high school students had been taught to think about research before they began their involvement in the Council of Youth Research. At that time, the term "research" conjured in their minds, as it has for many of us, visions of nameless, faceless scientists in white coats who sequestered themselves in laboratories and conducted complex experiments in order to make final pronouncements about what was "true" or "factual." As the result of an educational system that often locates the production of scientific knowledge away from and outside of local communities, the students did not feel that research connected meaningfully to their lives except through a vague sense that it was responsible for labeling their communities, their schools, and (often) themselves as "at risk" or "failing"; in turn, they were a bit perplexed about why they were involved in a program built around engaging in it.

Their misgivings are not difficult to understand; considering the variety of programs that exist to foster youth academic, socio-emotional, and civic development, involving activities from tutoring to the arts to community service, what do students gain by conducting research? Clearly, Dimitri and Evelyn's quotes suggest that something powerful happens when students feel that their personal experiences are valued and that they as young people can take on identities as experts. The potential of research to help young people feel empowered in this way demands further exploration.

This chapter aims to unpack the theoretical and epistemological history that provides the foundation for critical Youth Participatory Action Research (YPAR) as it was practiced in the Council and to provide the groundwork to explore this practice and its academic and social impacts. We will attend to the theoretical importance of youth, participation, and action to this practice but must begin by analyzing the assumptions behind the act of conducting research itself in order to draw out the qualities that make YPAR such a unique framework for fostering transformative outcomes for young people.

The Research Tradition

The Greek Philosophers and the Foundations of European Philosophy

While Dimitri and Evelyn's initial understanding of research—the idea that systematic collection and analysis of objective information from the world around us produces knowledge—seems commonplace today, this definition actually draws from particular understandings of what constitutes knowledge and how knowledge is created that have been developed and contested for much of recorded history.

The quest to understand the source of knowledge (and how individuals come to possess such knowledge) has occupied philosophers for centuries. Greek philosophers such as Plato did not ascribe to the view that the material world around us was a source of truth and knowledge; instead, he believed that true knowledge in the form of ideal abstractions existed innately within human beings and that humankind must use its faculties of analysis to look beyond the imperfect copies of material objects existing in the external world to recollect the knowledge contained within of original, perfect "Forms."

The distrust of the outside world as a source of knowledge that was manifested in Greek epistemology continued through the development of European philosophy, which turned overwhelmingly to religion as the wellspring of information needed to live a meaningful life and the inner source of truth. Following the fall of the Greek Empire in the first century BC, the dominant civilization in the West became what we now call the Roman Empire. While the Romans were innovators in many ways, they largely took their ideas about philosophy and epistemology from the Greeks. In AD 313 the Roman Emperor Constantine passed the Edict of Milan, essentially paving the way for the foundation of Christianity as the state religion and, from the 4th to 15th centuries in Europe, nearly all Western philosophers drew upon the Greek philosophical tradition to explain the major questions of the Christian faith. This is most exemplified in Thomas Aquinas, a 13th-century Scholastic philosopher whose major work, *Summa Theologica*, uses Aristotelian philosophy to prove the existence of God.

The Scientific Revolution

The 16th century witnessed many rapid and far-reaching changes. The invention of the Gutenberg printing press in the 15th century made knowledge easier to share. Advances in technology of travel made it possible to sail around the globe, ushering in the Age of Colonization (Principe, 2011). Many of the leading universities of Europe were creating departments that studied mathematics and science, and development in these fields ushered in what we now call the Scientific Revolution. Generally, the beginning of the Scientific Revolution is attributed to the publication of *On the Revolution of the Heavenly Spheres* by Nicolaus Copernicus in 1543, with its culmination coming in 1687 with the publication of Sir Isaac Newton's *Principia*.

One of the major figures of the Scientific Revolution is Sir Francis Bacon (1561–1626), who was a champion of empiricism. The empiricist model supports the belief that "true" knowledge can be gained only from particular kinds of inquiry in the world; namely, those based in science, with all of its attendant claims of objectivity. Looking at what he thought were shoddy and uneven methods of research in his time, Bacon called for a total reconstruction of sciences, arts, and all human knowledge. Bacon was primarily concerned with the method of knowledge production. The Baconian method, now more commonly known as the scientific method, involved rigorously testing hypotheses, experimentation, and the use of science to uncover general universal principles. These ideas are most clearly articulated in his 1620 publication, *Novum Organum*. Even though the formal conclusion of the Scientific Revolution occurred at the end of the 17th century, its ideas, its language, its epistemological values about what counts as knowing, and its connection of experimentation to the uncovering of universal truths largely remain with us through the tradition known as positivism.

The Rise of Positivism

Heavily inspired by the scientific revolution, John Locke (1632–1704) declared the human mind a "tabula rasa" in the late 17th century, further challenging the validity of internal knowledge while championing the value of the material world as a source of meaning. As an empiricist, Locke argued that humans are born as empty vessels and that they gain knowledge from sensory experience disciplined through the use of the scientific method (hence the image of scientists in lab coats collecting quantitative data). Instead of turning to an abstract or holy ideal, Locke put forth the idea that conducting rigorous analyses of the natural world elicits data that we can use to inform our actions.

Positivist philosophers like Auguste Comte extended the beliefs of empiricism into the 19th century. Beyond valuing sensory experience and the application of the scientific method, positivists stressed the idea that authoritative knowledge about the world could be gained through our senses only when filtered through logic and understanding of the inherent "laws" of society. As a result, positivists rejected intuitive knowledge or personal experience as a valid source of understanding.

Modernism, the Industrial Revolution, and the Age of Science

The ideas of Comte and positivism were greatly bolstered by the Industrial Revolution, which extended from the late 18th century through the 19th century. Some argue that the world witnessed more technological transformations during the period of 1750–1900 than it had in all of prior human history. Scientific advancements transformed methods of transportation, architecture, and the mass production of material goods. By the beginning of the 20th century, millions around the world were migrating from farms to work in factories in cities lined with skyscrapers. They communicated across oceans by telegraph. They travelled by steamships and railroads and enjoyed consumer goods that could now be produced by the millions. During this time science became associated with progress, advancement, and ultimate truth.

The positivist theory of knowledge acquisition guides much of what is considered valid scientific research up to the present day. Consider the federal government's insistence on providing funding almost exclusively for research projects that involve large-scale design experiments that promise objective, replicable results as opposed to small-scale, qualitative studies. Or consider the expansion of universities' offerings in the sciences while humanities programs struggle to defend their relevance. Nevertheless, the statements by Dimitri and Evelyn that opened this chapter speak to a different way of understanding and valuing knowledge—an inherent critique of the dominant research epistemology. Their critiques echo those made by Max Horkheimer and the philosophers of the Frankfurt School in the first decades of the 20th century.

The Response of Critical Theory

From the historic vantage points of the Great Depression and World War II, recently exiled from their native Germany as they watched the development of technologies that would make the destruction of the world possible (and would, in fact, lead to as many as 50 million war-related deaths in two decades), the Frankfurt School theorists questioned myths of human progress and enlightenment. These ideas would later cohere under the banner of critical theory and inspire intellectual and social movements that are still with us today. What binds these movements together is a distrust of grand narratives, of never-ending progress, and of objective, rational truths. Many of these early critical theorists witnessed firsthand the dangers associated with these myths and, through the massive destruction associated with the war, many came to reject the facile associations of scientific knowledge with ultimate truth. Intellectuals of the 1950s and 1960s did not only associate positivism with advances in medicine and industrial technology. There were also associations with atomic bombs, gas chambers, and massive oppression. It was then that the world began to take notice of these philosophers from the Frankfurt School who had been writing away in relative isolation since the late 1930s.

In their co-authored 1947 book, *The Dialectic of Enlightenment,* Frankfurt School philosophers Max Horkheimer and Ted Adorno critiqued the positivist assumption that society is structured by objective, immutable laws, instead stressing the socially constructed and mediated nature of what is taken for granted as "normal" or "dominant." They argued that what is seen as objective, in fact, represents the experience of those who possess more societal power, while the experiences of marginalized others are downplayed or outright ignored. Critical theorists pushed against the lack of attention paid to the consciousness of the observer in positivist models of knowledge creation and acquisition, just as our students pushed back against the idea that young people could not be seen as researchers or value their own experiences in school as valid data.

While empiricist and positivist epistemologies still predominate in social science research, a series of social and intellectual movements around the world have opened up crucial opportunities to interrogate the potentially oppressive assumptions guiding this model and introduce more socially just and critical ways of knowing, learning, and researching—ways that influence the theory, method, and practice of YPAR today. While doing justice to each movement would require more space than we have available in this book, we find it instructive to consider how some of these movements expanded the range of individuals and ideas that could *participate* in research—for example, feminism (women), postcolonialism (the colonized "other"), critical race studies (communities of color), postmodernism (historicity, discursiveness, and meta-analysis), and post-structuralism (instability of the structures that guide human thought and action).

YPAR emerges not only from this rich research tradition, but also from a series of social movements around the world as marginalized communities developed innovative ways to use research and knowledge production in order to organize and advocate for improved material and social conditions in society. We turn now to a review of several of these social movements in order to further interrogate the origins of the participatory and action elements of YPAR.

Theoretical Foundations of YPAR: A Study of Parallel Movements

As we acknowledge the rich theoretical tradition that informs YPAR, it is important to recognize that we are not simply noting a history of scholars working behind closed doors in isolated solitude. Behind the dense theory that may vex college students year after year lies a rich history of conflict, action, and human agency. Action begets theory, and we want to stress that the critical tradition from which YPAR emerges is built on the backs of social movements. In doing so, we offer a picture of revolutions and social tumult as not only the basis of how thinking develops in new ways, but also of the urgency with which scholars produce and theorize.

While we will introduce the Y of YPAR at the end of this chapter, we first want to consider the movements from the mid and late 20th century in which Participatory Action Research (PAR) was being developed in several locations around the world. Though certain similarities emerged as PAR was being developed across different contexts, there was not yet a unified methodology or even a fundamentally singular idea of "action research." By looking across theories of action being enacted in Britain, Latin America, and the United States, we offer one of the first accounts of how today's participatory action research model has built upon generations of work of activist-scholars toiling on the edges of critical theory. We begin by exploring British working-class action research. We then turn to an analysis of Latin American social movements of the 1960s. We will conclude with a discussion of pragmatism, and the contribution of the American civil rights movement to YPAR.

British Working-Class Action Research

Manic and surreal gunfire in the courtyard of a school concludes *If,* an ominous 1968 Lindsay Anderson film, the camera zooming in on the face of a young "everyman" (played by Malcolm McDowell) as he fires away deliriously at adult authority. To the clatter of gunshots, the film fades to black.

Though intentionally skipping between elements of fantasy and moments of school brutality and bullying, Anderson's film conveys the sense of in-school discontent that helped spark "action research" within England in the 1960s.

The action research model in England began in the mid-1960s as a response to upheaval within schools that was imaginatively addressed in Anderson's controversial film. The story of how this model of research came about in the mid '60s and beyond is one of in-school control, social upheaval, and empowerment of teachers. After an initial period of universal schooling, the educational system in Britain at the time diverged in the teenage years based on the concept of merit as determined by performance on national exams. As a result, a clear social divide persisted between high-achieving affluent students and general working-class youth. Educational researcher John Elliott (1991) described the situation:

> Grammar-school students . . . faced a choice of whether they left school for a job or proceeded to take certain GCE [General Certificate of Education] subjects for a further two years to secure advanced-level passes which together with their ordinary-level passes would secure entrance into a university. Those who failed the eleven-plus, the vast majority of students, followed a watered-down subject-based curriculum. A small proportion of these proceed to take GCE ordinary-level examinations at 16. The rest took either no public examinations at all or examinations which were considered to have inferior status to GCE. The national school-leaving age was 15, and many students left without taking any public examinations at all.
>
> *(p. 3)*

It is easy to imagine how large numbers of students in these schools felt "alienated from the 'watered-down' academic curriculum they followed" (p. 3).

This troubled portrait of working-class youth was corroborated by Paul Willis through his ethnographic research on youth during the early 1970s, captured in his 1977 book, *Learning to Labor*. His near-hopeless account of the educational trajectories of working-class "lads" is foretelling even in its opening sentences: "The difficult thing to explain about how middle-class kids get middle-class jobs is why others let them. The difficult thing to explain about how working-class kids get working-class jobs is why they let themselves" (p. 1). Willis's account illustrates the schooling mechanisms of control that establish working-class belief systems.

With high stakes testing functioning as sorting mechanism for British youth, the majority of students struggled to engage or find relevance in the public schooling system. As Elliott shared, "The alienation was particularly acute in those humanities subjects which students and their parents perceived to have little relevance to the world of work: namely, history, geography and religion." With students either passively tuned out of their schooling experiences or actively rebelling against them, teachers essentially had two choices. They could either further maintain schooling as a space for control or they could make school "intrinsically interesting" for students (Elliott, 1991, p. 9). It is out of the second of these two choices that the British form of action research emerges. As an example, in a 1968 article in *Journal of Curriculum Studies*, Lawrence Stenhouse (1968) outlines the "Humanities Curriculum Project" as having a specific purpose:

> To offer to schools and to teachers such stimulus, support and materials as may be appropriate to the mounting, as an element in general education

of enquiry-based courses, which cross the subject boundaries between English, history, geography, religious studies and social studies. The project is expected to concentrate on such support as will in particular meet the needs of adolescent pupils of average and below average academic ability.

(p. 26)

Stenhouse's description of this pioneering work of "action research" was staunchly "concerned with the content of education." In discussing "action research" from this perspective, we must recognize that this label is used to understand a curricular intervention deliberately applied to educational crises sweeping working-class schools across England. As such, "action research" in the 1960s and 1970s was related to democratizing teacher agency within classrooms and challenging the positivist notions of teacher professional development. Elliott summarized the key characteristic of this curricular work then newly labeled as "action research": "It is a process which is initiated by practising teachers in response to a particular practice situation they confront" (p. 9). Elliott highlighted the necessity for those closest to the classroom to engage with problems that could not be answered through adherence to traditional curricular practices by engaging in collaborative dialogic experimentation with alternative pedagogical strategies.

Notice that the focus of action research here is on teachers and the processes of teaching within classrooms. Though myriad scholars have added to this model of action research, Elliott offers a clear context for how the term formed and the purpose it serves: "The term 'action research' indicated a clarification of the research paradigm involved, and the relationship between research and teaching. They were not conceived as two separate activities" (p. 30). Fluidly seeing teaching as a kind of research and vice versa, action research was a pragmatic shift that increased teacher agency.

We want to note that this British model is built off of the pre-existing terminology. For scholars like Elliott and Stenhouse, "action research" was a term first used by Lewin (1946) to describe an iterative process of action, analysis, and further action. Lewin focused largely on organizational structures and dynamics which were picked up by British scholars looking at the aforementioned discontent in schools. This enactment of "action research" in the British context differed significantly from the South American tradition of action research that we will explore next.

What may seem to be missing in the British model of action research is the "research." Elliott contends that this is an intentional aspect: "The fundamental aim of action research is to improve practice rather than to produce knowledge. The production and utilization of knowledge is subordinate to, and conditioned by, the fundamental aim" (p. 49). In looking at the intentions of Stenhouse and Elliott as they enacted their vision of action research, it is clear that this is largely a model focused on teacher development. This approach focused on teachers being able to respond to and connect with the lived experiences of the students in their classroom from one day and one class to the next.

In terms of research and theory building, these were grounded in what took place within classrooms. Abstract notions of "theory building" make little sense in this model. Theory is contingent upon practical engagement with actual students. This model of action research is one that pushes against systematic forms of theory and teacher education. Instead, learning and "research" occur in response to in-class issues as they arise.

Further, although there is little direct response to positivism in the scholarship on this model of action research, the approach speaks clearly against singular approaches to research and knowledge production. By building knowledge *first* from the needs of teachers and their classes, we can see how assumptions of knowledge and research flip traditional stances within academies. Perhaps more importantly, by shifting how teachers learn and develop theory within their classrooms, this model of action research assumes learning to be an active and *new* process that can escape reproduction from one classroom to the next. The foundational tenets of positivism roughly chafe with the epistemological stance of focusing on teacher researchers.

While the British model of action research is one that can still be seen echoing across models of teacher inquiry today, there are several questions and limitations it brings to mind. For one, with classroom practice so contingent on teacher inquiry, what kinds of academic results were evaluated? Likewise, many of these British projects suffered from a lack of sustainability. Despite positioning theory and research and knowledge built outside of the walls of the academy, this model of action research was contingent on grant funding and university support. In numerous studies, the action research projects started by these scholars ended once funding ceased: maintaining teacher engagement without funding continued to be a challenge. As to be expected, the time demands on already busy teachers was a significant factor (Elliott p. 66).

Ultimately the models of participatory action research that were developed in working-class schools in England were less focused on liberation or critique of systems of oppression. Rather, they uprooted social structures that fomented dissatisfaction and disengagement within working-class schools. As such, we must question how different this model was from the prior stance of schooling as a means of control; in reflecting on the 1960s landscape of dissent and frustration fomenting within England's working-class schools, little is mentioned in the existing research on action research as to how such a model *improved* the life experiences of these youth beyond school. That is, did the students that participated in classrooms engaged in action research actually do measurably better than their peers? Regardless, we can trace from this movement the empowerment of teachers as researchers and a push for their voices to shape both research and curricular design in ways that will echo across the work of YPAR projects decades later.

Latin American Critical Theory and Resistance in Art, Schooling and Literacy

While YPAR borrows its name from the British action research movement of the 1960s, it is also heavily indebted to Latin American social movement theory of the 1970s. Most widely recognized in North America through the work of scholars like Paulo Freire (1921–1997), collectively these movements have helped to shape the way we think of teaching and learning (Freire, 1970), cultural production (Boal, 1979), and social science research (Morrow and Torres, 1995). At the heart of these movements is a real sense that the everyday individual must be involved in the remaking of the world. Moving beyond the critiques offered by critical theorists of the workings of power, Latin American social movement theory also considers the role of individual subjects in reclaiming ownership over their own narratives and playing active roles in changing their material world. At heart, this process involves a problem-posing education, the acquisition of dominant literacy practices, and participation in transformative dialogue and informed action (praxis) upon the world. Many of these ideas are associated with critical pedagogy and critical social theory, each of which we will explain in greater detail as they relate to our conceptualizing of the YPAR work.

Like many of the other scholars in this chapter, it is important to recognize that several of the figures acknowledged as leading a Latin American model of action research were themselves practitioners. Within the landscape of education, that Freire was first (and often foremost) a literacy *teacher* is underplayed. His work in educating and enacting what became known as his *Pedagogy of the Oppressed* (1970) is perhaps the legacy that overshadows the work that he did working face-to-face with students. The theories espoused in *Pedagogy of the Oppressed* emerged from over 20 years of work in very successful adult literacy movements in Brazil. For Freire, the most important component of the educational encounter was the true and authentic dialogue between the empowered human subject and the world. To speak is to name (or rename) the world. When learners are able to connect the words that matter most in their lives to the act of formal reading, reading the word becomes, literally, a reading of the world. We must first become literate in the language that allows us to reflect on our own existential experiences in the world (Freire & Macedo, 1987). And for those whose experiences include histories of oppression and marginalization, that act of literacy must also be tied to the work of personal and social emancipation.

Likewise, August Boal—whose similarly titled *Theater of the Oppressed* (1979) can be seen as an allied model of engagement within different social *spaces*—was himself an actor, writer, and director. Boal encouraged the use of theatre to both dramatize and work against oppression. Like Freire, Boal believed that theatre for historically marginalized groups should begin from their own experiences.

Rather than merely act out the famous plays of history, local communities should author their own plays. Even further, the act of performance should itself be a dialogue with the audience. In Boal's notions of forum theater, for instance, the audience could participate when witnessing acts of oppression on stage. They could suggest other possible actions or they could participate in the action and literally work toward change. In this way the dramatic performance constituted a critical dialogue and a social praxis. His work of practical exercises for developing an ethos of action within the theater, *Games for Actors and Non-Actors* (Boal, 1992), is written with little of the same theory that it drives toward; it is a book for working and for practice.

There are several aspects of the critical pedagogical theory of Freire and Boal that are important for our conception of YPAR. First, our work must begin with the everyday experiences of the students we work with. YPAR takes up the issues that matter most to the students, their schools, and their communities. Second, this work must be undertaken *with* students, not *for* them. A critical praxis is work in solidarity with youth. We cannot abandon our roles as adult educators, but neither can we do the work for the students. Third, the act of literacy is essential to the struggle. YPAR work must expose students to discourses of power so that they can effectively speak their truth to that power. And fourth, the act of literacy, or youth research, must be tied to acting upon (or renaming) the world to make it a more just, equitable, and humane place to inhabit.

Dewey, American Pragmatism, and the Foundations of YPAR

The current iteration of participatory action research that has taken hold in the American educational context is indebted not only to the British tradition and Latin American social movements, but also to homegrown philosophy about the nature and purpose of knowledge in a democratic society.

Whereas critical theorists of the Frankfurt School responded to the exclusionary aspects of positivism and empiricism with a healthy distrust of the power of the scientific process to foster social progress, a group of early 20th century American philosophers led by Charles Peirce, William James, and John Dewey maintained faith in the scientific process but aimed to make it more inclusionary and responsive to a complex society that did not always operate according to tidy logical propositions.

They argued that positivism erected too high of a barrier between thought and the world—that the preoccupation with logic in the workings of the mind led to the erroneous idea that truth could be found in the abstract apart from the messy workings of the real world. Under the banner of pragmatism, these philosophers argued instead that any idea had to be considered provisional until it had circulated in society and been found useful in providing a basis for human action in that society. In essence, pragmatists argued that true knowledge could only be developed through the interactions between individuals—it existed only in the world as it is, not in the abstract landscape of the mind.

And more importantly for Dewey, knowledge in a truly democratic society had to emerge from dialogue between individuals of equal status and value in the world. In his landmark 1916 book, *Democracy and Education*, Dewey stated that "democracy is more than a form of government; it is primarily a mode of associated living, of conjoint communicated experience" (p. 101). Dialogue defined democracy for Dewey as the essence of shared collective life; as he explained, "Society not only continues to exist by transmission, by communication, but it may fairly be said to exist in transmission, in communication" (p. 5). In other words, communication is not a precondition for democracy—the process embodies democracy itself.

Nevertheless, Dewey recognized that American society in the early 20th century was characterized by extreme inequalities by race and class, threatening the democratic ideal. Sociologist W.E.B. Du Bois powerfully exposed the paradoxical experience of being both an American and an African-American in a systemically unequal society; as he explained in 1903 in *The Souls of Black Folk*, "One ever feels his twoness—an American, a Negro; two souls, two thoughts, two unreconciled strivings; two warring ideals in one dark body, whose dogged strength alone keeps it from being torn asunder" (p. 5). Du Bois illustrates the painful reality of a democracy in which an entire race was excluded from the democratic conversation.

In *The Public and Its Problems* (1927), Dewey called for a process of participatory social inquiry to explore and remedy the ills of democracy in which ordinary citizens could come together in what he termed "The Great Community" to share knowledge and develop means of addressing seemingly intractable social problems. As he maintained, "the cure for the ailments of democracy is more democracy" (p. 146). He believed that researchers and other experts had a role to play in contributing to these conversations, but a limited one that must engage with the experience of the wider public who had firsthand experience of the problems at hand. He insisted that the spirit of experimentation and the use of scientific research methods could help citizens use inquiry to create a more equitable world.

Dewey's ideas contribute to current understandings of YPAR not only by highlighting the need to honor knowledge production from all corners of society (in YPAR's case, young people), but also through envisioning university researchers and other traditionally defined experts as public intellectuals with a responsibility to work with community members to improve society. And, of course, the overarching idea of seeing society as it is and seeking to make it more democratic and just is a priority of YPAR.

Nevertheless, some philosophers in the African-American pragmatist tradition maintain that Dewey and other early pragmatists never fully engaged with the effects of systemic racism and oppression on democracy. Cornel West (1989) criticized traditional pragmatism for being aware of the exclusion of people of color and women from democracy, but remaining "fearful of the subversive demands that these excluded people might make and enact" (5). And in *A Shade of Blue: Pragmatism and the Politics of Black America*, Eddie Glaude argues that Dewey "never addressed racism as a central challenge to democracy" (39).

These philosophers contributed to the pragmatist tradition by insisting that the public contend with America's legacy of racism in order to more fully approach democratic ideals. Indeed, African-American activists had already taken up this challenge during the civil rights movement by engaging in the types of radical education work that inform current YPAR efforts. For instance, Freedom Schools, established across the state of Mississippi during the "Freedom Summer" of 1964 through the combined efforts of the four major civil rights organizations, aimed to empower Black Americans to engage in the political struggle for power through social inquiry.

These 41 summer schools, which convened everywhere from churches to fields and were run mostly by college student volunteers, aimed to present their students, young and old alike, with lessons in confidence, voter literacy, and political organization skills as the basis for the formation of a new, mixed-race political party that could counter the all-white Mississippi political establishment. While the Freedom Schools did teach academic skills that students were not being exposed to in some segregated schools, their primary focus was the "Citizenship Curriculum," a set of unit plans designed to relate students' personal experiences to the larger political structure around them as a catalyst for social action.

The American civil rights movements can be seen as useful parallels to Latin American social movements as forebears of YPAR in promoting the ideas that education and research production should be put to the purpose of giving a voice to disenfranchised populations and agitating for social justice. They highlight the need for marginalized communities to engage in their own processes of knowledge production and dissemination as forms of social and political empowerment and insist that dominant power structures recognize the social and cultural capital of communities of color. While traditional views of cultural capital advanced by philosophers like Pierre Bourdieu (1986) maintain that the knowledges of upper and middle classes are the only ones considered valuable forms of cultural exchange in unequal societies, critical educational researchers like Tara Yosso (2005) criticize these views for encouraging a deficit view of low-income communities of color and instead highlight their strengths as Community Cultural Wealth.

Within this tradition, YPAR can be seen as a strategy to help young people develop critical capital and share their knowledge with society in order to agitate for social justice.

Current YPAR Research: Focusing on Youth

The emergence of YPAR as a method for educational research over the past 15 years is informed by each of these research traditions and the complex theoretical history of research itself. Importantly, it is also informed by education policy and by educational theories that emerge from the critical research tradition that finally introduce the all-important Y of YPAR.

Dewey's argument that knowledge is created in the social interactions between individuals in cultural contexts implies the need for pedagogy grounded in dialogue and shared inquiry; however, in today's educational climate, knowledge and pedagogy are treated in drastically different ways. As Cochran-Smith and Lytle (2006) explain, current policy conceptualizes knowledge as discrete chunks of information to be recalled on demand for the purpose of high-stakes testing; this leads to a conceptualization of "good" teaching as simply the ability to raise test scores through the use of materials geared toward that narrow purpose. In addition to contributing to a narrowing of the purpose of schooling, this also contributes to a simplified conceptualization of teaching preparation, practice, and professional development (p. 680). Teacher learning is replaced by training in the techniques believed to transmit nuggets of content and raise test scores, just as student learning is replaced by the accumulation of content knowledge and test preparation.

According to much recent critical social theory, the high-stakes accountability movement reflects the larger neoliberal project aimed at reproducing oppressive race and class structures (Apple, 2006). When following the market logic, teachers of the working class are charged with preparing a population that, according to many reproduction theorists, are being prepared to take working-class jobs (MacLeod, 1987).

As we introduced earlier in the chapter, Freire's model of critical pedagogy has emerged as an alternative vision of teaching and learning of young people that challenges social reproduction by using dialogue to spur individual and collective social transformation. Teachers, in this model, do not teach students; instead, teachers and students educate each other in a dialogic relationship aimed at understanding the world and then acting upon it to humanize both the oppressors and the oppressed. Theorists who have extended Freire's ideas about critical pedagogy have focused on how to apply its tenets to classroom practice in ways that disrupt the process of social reproduction and re-define the relationship between teachers and students. Henry Giroux (1988) introduces the concept of "liberating memory" as one that can bring teachers and students together in solidarity through the shared remembrance of suffering (p. xxxiv). Peter McLaren (1995) stresses the need for students and teachers to analyze schools as political sites characterized by asymmetrical power relations as a starting point for revolutionary action. And Ira Shor (1992) introduces the concept of "critical-democratic pedagogy for self and social change" (p. 15) by presenting case studies of classrooms grounded in eight values of "empowering education": participatory, affective, situated, problem-posing, multicultural, dialogic, desocializing, and democratic learning. All stress the importance of genuine, critical dialogue to the enactment of democratic relationships in schools.

These ideas of critical pedagogy have meshed with the ideas of critical research and the history of social movements and given rise to YPAR as we know it today. A number of educational scholars engaging in YPAR today ground their research by, for, and with young people in some amalgam of these intersecting traditions (see Akom, 2009; Cammarota & Romero, 2011; Duncan-Andrade & Morrell, 2008; Fine & Cammarota, 2008; Irizarry, 2011; Kirshner, 2010; McIntyre, 2000; Stovall & Delgado, 2009; Yang, 2009).

While these scholars engage in a range of activities with students and study a variety of topics in various geographic locations, they are united by a commitment to engaging low-income youth of color in the YPAR process and challenging the dominant epistemological and methodological understandings of research explored in this chapter. Our work with the Council complements theirs, and we tell our story in the following chapters in order to demonstrate the specific ways in which our project responded to and extended the YPAR tradition.

References

Akom, A. A. (2009). Critical hip hop pedagogy as a form of liberatory praxis. *Equity & Excellence in Education, 42*(1), 52–66.

Apple, M. W. (2006). *Educating the "right" way: Markets, standards, God, and inequality (2nd ed.)*. New York: Routledge.

Boal, A. (1979). *Theatre of the oppressed*. London: Pluto Press.

Boal, A. (1992). *Games for actors and non-actors*. London: Routledge.

Bourdieu, P. (1986). The forms of capital. In J. Richardson (Ed.), *Handbook of theory and research for the sociology of education* (241–258). New York: Greenwood.

Cammarota, J., & Romero, A. (2011). Participatory action research for high school students: Transforming policy, practice, and the personal with social justice education. *Educational Policy, 25*(3), 488–506.

Cochran-Smith, M., & Lytle, S. (2006). Troubling images of teaching in No Child Left Behind. *Harvard Educational Review, 76*(4), 668–697.

Dewey, J. (1916). *Democracy and education; an introduction to the philosophy of education.* New York: The Macmillan Company.

Dewey, J. (1927). *The public and its problems.* New York: H. Holt and Company.

Du Bois, W.E.B. (1903). *The souls of black folk.* New York: Modern World Library.

Duncan-Andrade, J. M. R., & Morrell, E. (2008). *The art of critical pedagogy: Possibilities for moving from theory to practice in urban schools.* New York: Peter Lang.

Elliott, J. (1991). *Action research for educational change.* Buckingham: Open University Press.

Fine, M., & Cammarota, J. (2008). *Revolutionizing education: Youth participatory action research in motion.* New York: Routledge.

Freire, P. (1970). *Pedagogy of the oppressed.* New York: Seabury Press.

Freire, P., & Macedo, D. (1987). *Literacy: Reading the word and the world.* Westport: Bergin and Garvey.

Giroux, H. A. (1988). *Schooling and the struggle for public life.* Minneapolis: University of Minnesota Press.

Glaude, E. (2007). *In a shade of blue: Pragmatism and the politics of black America.* Chicago: Chicago University Press.

Horkheimer, M., & Adorno, T. (1947/1969). *The dialectic of enlightenment.* New York: Continuum.

Irizarry, J. (2011). Buscando la libertad: Latino youths in search of freedom in school. *Democracy & Education, 19*(1), 1–10.

Kirshner, B. (2010). Productive tensions in youth participatory action research. *Yearbook of the National Society for the Study of Education, 109*(1), 238–251.

Lewin, K. (1946). Action research and minority problems. In G.W. Lewin (Ed.), *Resolving social conflicts.* New York: Harper & Row, 201–216.

MacLeod, J. (1987). *Ain't no makin' it: leveled aspirations in a low-income neighborhood.* Boulder, Colo.: Westview Press.

McIntyre, A. (2000). Constructing meaning about violence, school, and community: Participatory action research with urban youth. *The Urban Review, 32*(2), 123–154.

McLaren, P. (1995). *Critical pedagogy and predatory culture.* New York: Routledge.

Morrow, R., & Torres, C. (1995). *Social theory and education: A critique of theories of social and cultural reproduction.* Albany: SUNY Press.

Principe, L. M. (2011). *The scientific revolution: A very short introduction.* Oxford: Oxford University Press.

Shor, I. (1992). *Empowering education.* Chicago: University of Chicago Press.

Stenhouse, L. (1968). The humanities curriculum project. *Journal of Curriculum Studies, 1*(1), 26–33.

Stovall, D., & Delgado, N. (2009). "Knowing the ledge": Participatory action research as legal studies for urban high school youth. *New Directions for Youth Development, 123,* 67–81.

West, C. (1989). *The American evasion of philosophy: A genealogy of pragmatism.* Madison: University of Wisconsin Press.

Yang, K. W. (2009). Mathematics, critical literacy, and youth participatory action research. *New Directions for Youth Development, 123,* 99–118.

Yosso, T. (2005). Whose culture has capital? A critical race theory discussion of community cultural wealth. *Race, Ethnicity and Education, 8*(1), 69–91.

FIGURE 1 Members of the 2009 summer seminar cohort pass the torch to the next generation of Council students at the 2010 summer seminar presentation at Los Angeles City Hall

FIGURE 2 Council students conduct interviews out in the field during the 2010 summer seminar

INTERLUDE

Discussing the Council's Origins

In this conversation, Nicole and Antero talk to Council of Youth Research co-founders Ernest Morrell and John Rogers about the epistemologies and methodologies that informed the Council from its beginnings in 1999 through the 2010–2011 school year. The discussion highlights the ways that Ernest and John drew from critical theories of learning, identity, and power to create an innovative, youth-led learning environment.

Nicole: I'm wondering about the kinds of conversations that the two of you had as the Council developed and how your ideas meshed to create something unique.

John: Let me say two things. One is that there certainly was this stream in the early Council work that I think was partially Deweyan but had a broader set of antecedents as well. The other thing I wanted to say was that starting around 1999 we were diving into Bourdieu and thinking about the ways that the work we were doing offered an extension of Bourdieu's framework. Ernest and I developed a framework for critical capital as a way to capture the deep work that was being done.

Ernest: There was an approach that I saw happening at UCLA that was very different than what I had experienced [while I was a student at] Berkeley. Then there were the ideas that were unique that I felt I was bringing from Berkeley. The UCLA scholars were heavily into critical learning theory; they were drawing upon Lave and Wenger's situated cognition theory in really powerful ways. I didn't have that learning theory to go along with the critical pedagogical theory we were exploring at Berkeley. We were really heavily steeped in Antonio Gramsci and Michael Apple and counter-hegemony, but how does that happen? We didn't have a strong theory of learning as legitimate peripheral participation. When I came to UCLA we participated in a reading group bridging Dewey's social theory of education with Lave and Wenger's social theory of learning. Together with Freire's ideas about humanizing education as praxis, this formed what I believe was a really powerful set of ideas that have a lot to do with how the summer seminar was set up and what it meant for us for youth to participate in research in powerful ways.

What does legitimate peripheral participation in a community of researchers mean? In some ways I think that's a more sophisticated idea than youth participatory action research. We were not thinking about this as something young people do; we were thinking about apprenticing young people into a community of researchers that involved adults and professionals and Ph.Ds. So moving from legitimate peripheral participation to core participation didn't just mean you were becoming an expert in YPAR; it meant that you were becoming an authentic participant in the community of critical sociologists. That was, I think, one of the core sets of ideas that's really important when you think about adult/youth interactions. The language of youth participatory action research came to us after that—that was really 2005–2007; you see it in Julio Cammarota and Michelle Fine's work. We were calling it critical research. We were calling it *a critical research in education.*

John: That's right.

Ernest: Those sorts of terms were what we were wrapping our minds around. Now, one of the ideas that I think was really important to sink our teeth into was—many educators had been engaging Paulo Freire's critical pedagogical theory, but at that time the consensus of Peter [McLaren], [Henry] Giroux, and others in the late '90s was that this theory had no place in schools. This was about transforming society. Schools were envisioned as neoliberal institutions where none of this critical work could happen. So a lot of the translation of critical theory into K–12 spaces was about developing a language of critique, but not necessarily praxis.

In the work that Jeff [Duncan-Andrade] and I had been doing in our high school classrooms while we were studying at Berkeley, young people had been developing a critical voice. They were able to articulate their conditions but there wasn't really a space for us to act upon that. They would be analyzing an advertisement and discussing ways that media representations were racist or sexist and we were saying, "that's critical," but it wasn't praxis. What praxis would look like is when we were working with young people who are actually advocating for their own conditions. Our Council of Youth Research work was possible because it occurred outside of the spaces of schooling and there wasn't a formal curriculum that we had to adhere to. But those were ideas that really began to take flight in the summer seminar space. We began to talk about it as an academic space but not a school space. What would it mean to really center it around problem-posing education? What would it mean to involve young people in this process? What would it mean to create participatory learning structures that were very different from the very didactic approach that was happening in schools? I saw those as the core ideas coming together.

The other idea that John began to talk about was capital theory and I still think we were pushing on capital theory in a way that was different than the emerging binary in the sociology of education between the work of Pierre Bourdieu and Tara Yosso. Bourdieu analyzes dominant cultural capital as an explanatory model for the inequitable distribution of resources in society. Tara Yosso's scholarship illuminates alternate forms of capital that exist largely in marginalized and nondominant populations. We formulated a synthesis of the two—or at least a dialectic of the two. That leads to: how do you leverage young people's intimate connection to their community to facilitate a navigational capital that allows them to speak to and participate within dominant structures? We were calling that critical capital. The funds of knowledge scholarship and capital theory of Moll and Yosso do not solve the problem of how young people navigate power and speak to power. Their work speaks quite profoundly to the necessity of honoring nondominant cultural practices, but it's not about leveraging dominant forms of capital per se in the way that Bourdieu feels is necessary for social transformation, so we were really adamant about having both. Is it possible to make this connection between young people becoming advocates on their own behalf but also them leveraging a different kind of capital that also has power in the dominant sphere, whether that's access to college, whether that's impacting policy, having an authentic voice in the public domain?

John Rogers: If I can just pick up on a couple of things there, I think that one of the central tenets of Bourdieu's capital theory is that capital and symbolic capital become a way to reproduce inequalities because of monopolies that are held over knowledge. What we saw in critical capital was an opportunity to undermine that monopoly because you are saying that not just elites of a particular sort have access to knowledge and to the tools of investigation, but that young people from communities being negatively impacted by inequality also have access to those tools and can shape the knowledge-making process. The other idea that was tied to capital theory, which I think is a huge insight for YPAR, was that there needed to be opportunities to change the markets of exchange.

What I mean by this is that inside of schools, the only markets of exchange really are the grade processes—students produce some type of work and teachers have control over giving value to that work. In the context of our seminars, we tried to construct opportunities for valuable exchange where young people could share their work with those who had the power to effect political and institutional change and to give human value to the work that the young people were doing. I think that insight proved to be really important because we saw that when students went back to their school settings out of the summer seminar, they didn't have these markets of exchange, and these empowered young people could be diminished by those institutional sites.

One last thing. At one point, in trying to make sense of this, Ernest and I developed this triangle, which was an attempt to condense that which distinguished the powerful learning space of the summer seminar context from the oftentimes disempowering context of regular classrooms. The triangle included activities on one of the vertices, work products that students produced on another, and the different participants in this space on the third. In large measure, we were struck by the fact that many of the activities the young people engaged in in an English Language Arts classroom were not all that dissimilar from what they engaged in in the context of this more empowering space. The participants were somewhat different in that they included not just teachers and students, but many of these others as well. That was critically important to understanding why this space was far more powerful. And then the work products also were both similar and different—they were different in the sense that students had ownership of them. It was the relationship between these three pieces that was really different in the summer seminar.

Antero:	I'm curious about where these discussions were happening—the conversation about Bourdieu versus Yosso, for example. I'm assuming that some of these conversations were happening in the readings students were doing, but part of this was much more about the theoretical framing around how this work is being done among the adult researchers. Could you parse out which conversations were happening where?
Ernest:	Definitely, the questions about power and about critical theories were conversations in both spaces. Very early on, the students would have been seriously engaging Paulo Freire's and Antonio Gramsci's scholarship and thinking about the importance of people whose voices had been traditionally marginalized from power—what we might call now the importance of speaking truth to power. That young people, people of color, people living in central cities were often marginalized from those conversations and because of that were acted upon as objects instead of subjects would have been a part of all of our conversations with the young people from the

very beginning. Bourdieu as well, I think, because his was a theory that we were connecting not only with young people navigating dominant capital, but as a way of explaining why certain people's knowledges were valued above others. Some of the meta-conversations about learning via social inquiry or via legitimate peripheral participation—those were conversations we were having as an adult group of researchers, like the reading of Lave & Wenger. But all of those dialogues about critical sociology were a part of the shared conversation. I think that there were a couple of summers where the class was actually titled "The Critical Sociology of Education."

FIGURE 3 The Council group that explored powerful curriculum presents their research questions

3

THE PEDAGOGY OF RELATIONSHIPS AS THE CORE OF YPAR

I couldn't sleep last night. How could I stop my brain from racing when the summer seminar was about to begin?

I was still buzzing from the planning meetings last week—the passionate conversations among our teacher leaders about the shared purpose of our work, the lightning-fast brainstorming about the resources and networks in Los Angeles that we will engage to enrich our students' learning, and the careful planning for the culminating presentation that will take place just five short weeks from now (eeek!).

At the same time, I was charged with anticipation as I looked forward to meeting the 30 individual students who I know will soon coalesce into a tight-knit community of young researchers.

Even as I lay awake in bed, I predicted how the day would begin. I would lug cartloads of supplies across the UCLA campus to the law school classroom that will serve as our home base for the summer and carefully put all of the logistics in order. Name tags at every seat, bus tokens separated into bundles for each student, campus meal cards ready to be distributed.

Students will start to arrive around 8:30 a.m., shyly sticking closely to other students from their schools as they recount stories of learning new bus routes from South L.A. to UCLA and getting lost on the way to our building. Some will be superstars at their schools, accustomed to achieving amid struggle and curious about what this next summer enrichment program will be about. Others will be less comfortable in the academic environment, persuaded to come and test out this group by teachers who recognized a spark in them that needed to be teased out. Everyone will be hesitant, unsure what to expect.

The teachers and graduate students will filter in, and the level of happy noise will rise in the room as they reunite with their students after several weeks of vacation and with the fellow adults who they last saw days or weeks or months ago. I will review the agenda for the day one last time and prepare the icebreaker activities that will help us to relax into this space with each other so that we can lay the groundwork for the journey ahead of us.

The room will buzz with potential. And this potential is what propelled me out of bed extra early this morning, because I simply can't wait to begin building with this community.

As we discussed in the last chapter, YPAR has emerged at the intersection of many social and educational theories, which means that those who "do" YPAR may approach their practice from varying ideological standpoints and carry out their research in very different ways. In the chapters that follow, we will explain and analyze what YPAR meant in the specific context of the Council of Youth Research. But before we delve into what made the Council unique in its pedagogy of research, we find it crucial to devote attention to one thing that unites YPAR programs regardless of their theoretical and practical orientations—their pedagogies of relationships.

Nicole wrote the vignette above on the first day of the 2010 Summer Seminar, aiming to capture the unique learning environment that the Council offered and the feelings of excitement, comfort, and anticipation that it inspired. We believe that while the resources brought to bear and the activities that the group planned and engaged in contributed to this learning environment, the core of what made the Council a revolutionary learning space was the love generated among the group—a bond that transcended any one member and existed only in the power of the collective.

One constant across the YPAR research that we have combed through is the practice of doing YPAR within group settings. Of course, research in general is often a social practice involving relationships among researchers and between researchers and participants, but YPAR is unique in the way that it conceptualizes participation—as not simply the act of working in concert with others, but as the formation of strong relational bonds and the development of community that serve as prerequisites for engaging in any part of the research cycle.

In this chapter, we will examine the crucial role that relationships play in YPAR generally as foundations for teaching and learning in communities of practice. We will then detail the unique pedagogy of relationships in the Council that supported a community of adult and student learners. Along the way we will point out the ways that this pedagogy speaks back to many taken-for-granted understandings about how adults and youth should interact in both formal and informal academic settings.

YPAR and Communities of Practice

As we highlighted in our discussion of the American YPAR tradition in Chapter 2, relationships are central to democratic, participatory forms of learning. Humans are social animals—we do not exist (or learn) by ourselves in social and cultural vacuums. Instead, as socio-cultural theories of learning remind us, we learn through interactions with others that are shaped by the specific times and places in which they occur, as well as tools we use to engage in our shared activities (Rogoff, 2003; Vygotsky, 1978). As a result, everything we know emerges from relationships. We may see ourselves as individuals, but our identities are inextricably linked to those of the people we talk, laugh, and think with throughout our lives.

Researchers Jean Lave and Etienne Wenger (1991) used the term "community of practice" to describe groups of people engaged in collective learning around a shared purpose. They explain how new members in such groups learn community practices by slowly increasing their levels of participation in shared cultural practices, with help from scaffolding provided by more experienced members, until they themselves become core participants, in a process of "legitimate peripheral participation." Community is key to this concept because it is through joint participation that members of the community gain expertise; the end goal is not simply to acquire knowledge or skills, but to acquire "identities of mastery."

We'd like to describe how the Council of Youth Research has developed over time into a community of practice dedicated to youth empowerment and social change, beginning with the adult members and extending outward to include student researchers.

Starting with the Adults: The Council of Youth Research as a Community of Practice

At the start of the summer of 2008, a few months before Nicole would begin the Urban Schooling doctoral program at UCLA, she asked her new advisor, John Rogers, if she could volunteer with the Council of Youth Research summer seminar. She had read about the program and was eager to get involved as a way to stay engaged with young people after leaving the classroom. John invited her to observe, and so began her years-long plunge into the world of YPAR, first as a graduate student researcher and eventually as the coordinator of the program.

It wasn't until years had passed and her involvement in the Council had long been solidified that Nicole learned from Ernest, with much laughter, that he had originally had major reservations about allowing her to observe that first summer. His reason? He was so protective of the Council community that he was wary of allowing adults to join without being completely sure of their levels of commitment to the students and to the work. Was this new graduate student going to stay committed to the students for the long haul, or was she just going to get involved in order to pad her resume and then move on? Did she know how to relate to youth in this type of setting? Ernest didn't know, and so he was cautious.

This story, particularly the questions that swirled around in Ernest's head as he considered a new adult joining the Council community, speaks to how necessary relational trust between adults was (and is) to sustaining the group and how carefully the adults in the Council managed the group in order to create that trust. Anthony Bryk and Barbara Schneider (2004) define relational trust as the interpersonal relationships and mutual dependencies that connect actors within educational environments and make possible the vulnerability and openness needed for meaningful learning. Before we could even consider what it would take to build this trust between adults and youth in the Council, we had to ensure that trust existed among the adults themselves.

Adult trust developed in several ways. One of the most powerful was the shared connection that the group members had; in this case, the connection to the UCLA Graduate School of Education and the Los Angeles Unified School District (LAUSD). Of the five core teachers that led school groups with the Council during the 2010–2011 school year, four attended UCLA's Teacher Education Program (TEP), and the fifth joined us at the recommendation of her principal, another TEP alumnus. As large as LAUSD is, this group of teachers knew each other or knew *of* each other before working together with the Council, either through taking classes together or through social networks with other TEP alumni.

These TEP connections were important not only because the teachers shared the same teacher credentialing experience and met Ernest and John at UCLA, but also because the program encouraged teachers to place social justice at the center of their practice. Of TEP's eight guiding principles, the first is to "embody a social justice agenda," and while the program encouraged all teachers to come to their own understandings of social justice, the Council teachers developed a common collective vision and vocabulary of social justice teaching through their involvement with the Council. Fred, our teacher from Crenshaw High School, expressed some elements of this common vision as he described how his colleagues often viewed his work with the group:

> It's funny, somebody had brought that up, like, it's so commendable what you're doing. I'm like, nah, man, it's not that commendable. I'm not doing anything different than someone who's aware and understands the reality of this awareness. It's out of necessity. It's no question that that commitment to a certain population of students is needed. These commitments from everybody else have fallen short. Somebody's gotta break that cycle. So I just feel like staying late, doing all this stuff that we do after the bell. If you understand the community that you teach in, you understand the experiences and conditions that your students go through every day and lack of opportunities that are available to them, then why aren't you? We're situated as teachers in a position where we can at least create these spaces for them. I just think that especially as someone who is informed, someone who is critical, someone who is aware, you have to realize the reality of all this and how it really plays out into what we see in the classroom. Gotta do this, you know what I mean?

Fred's commitment was echoed by his colleagues, which created a bond of solidarity that spurred the work of the Council forward. While institutional connections and shared values can help to provide the initial connections between educators, the process of becoming a true community of practice is simultaneously much more organic and much more painstakingly planned. Issues of leadership, power, and resources must be constantly negotiated and renegotiated as a community coalesces.

Relationship-Building in the Council: Summer of 2010

In a conscious commitment to fostering adult relationship-building, the Council upheld a tradition of bringing the teachers from participating schools together for short retreats before the summer seminars began to reconnect and set the stage for the student research to come. In the summer of 2010, the 2-day retreat focused on the research frame, "The State of Education 10 Years After *Williams*." As described in Chapter 1, Ernest and John developed this research frame on the 10-year anniversary of the *Williams v. California* case filing in order to inject student voices into a discussion of how urban schools had (or had not) changed since the decision.

A quick note about the adult role in the youth research process is in order here. It may seem contrary to the spirit of YPAR for adults to set up a research frame to guide students' work; after all, shouldn't youth be in charge of every aspect of the research in order for it to be truly considered youth-led? While it may seem that adult involvement in YPAR takes away from youth agency, we have found through our work that adults have a crucially important role to play in facilitating the research process; that, indeed, their active mentoring and support actually bolsters youth agency. Setting young people off on a research project without access to the resources, knowledge, and relationships that adults can provide can do a disservice to YPAR by denying students the necessary tools to reap the full benefits of the process.

As discussed in the introduction, Ernest and John knew that the ten-year anniversary of the *Williams* filing would garner media attention, providing the opportunity for Council students to offer young people's perspectives on this timely issue. They also knew that they could leverage connections they had with legislators and policymakers around the state, including in the state capital of Sacramento, in order to supply students with potential interviewees, a ready-made audience, and the most recent data for their research. While they, and all of the adults that worked with the Council, knew that our students were capable of far more self-directed learning and critical thought than they were often given opportunities to demonstrate in school, they also never forgot the responsibility of the adults in the program to build relationships among themselves and with their social networks so that they could be the best possible teachers to guide them.

The retreat functioned as both a time to strengthen relationships and an opportunity to allow the research theme to develop organically based on the interests, expertise, and connections that the teachers brought to the table. At the end of June, the teachers gathered around a table in the conference room of UCLA's Institute for Democracy, Education, and Access, just a short walk from the UCLA Law School where the students would soon gather for the Summer Seminar, and they talked excitedly about their plans for their students over the next six weeks. Behind them, colorful murals featured images of John Dewey and Ella Baker watching over their work.

The teacher team used the retreat as a time to build relationships as they each found their own niche within the research theme for the year. First, they brainstormed the elements that they found most important to measure in order to present a clear portrait of the state of education in Los Angeles high schools, and after batting around a number of ideas, decided that the major building blocks of quality education were high-quality teaching, powerful leadership, engaging curriculum, sufficient learning resources, and a healthy social and physical environment. At this point, they began friendly jockeying to decide which of these five research areas each of them would choose as their focus.

Much of this decision-making process revolved around the resources and relationships that the teachers thought they could bring to the table to provide the most enriching experience for their students. For instance, Maria knew that she could draw upon her experiences with the National Board Teacher Certification process and the TEP program to help students think about the most important elements of a quality teacher. She also knew that she could reach out to administrators at her school as potential interviewees for students as they learned about how principals evaluated teachers. As a result, she emerged as the leader for the Teaching research area.

Similarly, LT drew upon his connections with administrators from across the Los Angeles Unified School District, as well as then–District Superintendent Ray Cortines, to take ownership of the Leadership research area. He found himself drawn by the question of how leaders approached issues of inequity in their schools and in the city and excitedly imagined the folks he could introduce students to from community schools and the UCLA Principal Leadership Institute.

Teachers drew upon their networks not only to plan opportunities in their research areas, but also to bring together panels of speakers who could help students learn about the landscape of education in the city so that their eventual research questions and data collection could be as robust and sophisticated as possible. While they thought it was important for students to meet and talk with adults traditionally considered educational leaders, including principals and school board members, they also found it crucial for students to hear the perspectives of community organizations and fellow students.

As a result, they reached out to members of groups that they belonged to or knew well—groups that they trusted to provide students with nuanced perspectives and, most importantly, that they knew could relate well to young people. For instance, they reached out to Parent U-Turn, a group of parents committed to giving family members a seat at the table of education reform, as well as Inner City Struggle, a youth organizing group that worked in the same neighborhoods in which our students went to school.

The process of planning the summer seminar demonstrated the integral role that adult relationships play in setting up the conditions and community within which YPAR can be most successful. In order to prepare young people for the academic and socio-emotional demands of critical research and encourage them to go out on a limb and push themselves to become civic agents of change, adults bore a responsibility to provide the most supportive environment possible— one that would be ready to pick them up when they faltered and open new opportunities for them as they tapped into potential some of them never realized they possessed. This environment had to be carefully built upon a foundation of trust and love and respect for young people among all participants—teachers, professors, graduate students, and community members. Only then could young people be welcomed into this safe space and become apprentices in this community of practice.

The Start of Summer Seminar: Welcoming Youth into the Community

Civic Identity and Caring

Before we consider that the Council involves participatory action research, we find it important to recognize that the Council was first and foremost a youth program and to clarify how adult members conceptualized their goals for youth development. Many after-school and summer programs work with high school youth with the aim of exposing them to a variety of activities (i.e., arts, technology) in order to promote academic success, prosocial behaviors, and creative expression. Whether directly or indirectly, many such programs draw from positive youth development theory, which emerged in the 1990s as an assets-based view of adolescents aimed at countering negative portrayals of teens as dangerous or "at-risk" (Larson, 2000).

Indeed, many of the goals that adults had for Council students as they planned the 2010 Summer Seminar drew from positive youth development theory and were aimed at preparing young people for positive academic and social/emotional trajectories through high school and into post-secondary education. They wanted young people to increase their academic literacy skills through reading complex informational texts; to learn how to work together with young people and adults in various contexts; to develop strategies for overcoming setbacks; to experience life on a college campus; and to hone their communication and presentation skills, among many other goals.

But they were also aiming for something more, and this desire is what led to YPAR. As we discussed in Chapter 2, PAR has historically been employed as a way for individuals and groups to analyze the social, historical, economic, and political contexts in which they live and take action to inject marginalized voices into public discourse and redress inequities. It is about seeing young people not simply as individuals, but as a group of developing citizens. As a result, choosing to engage in PAR with low-income youth of color attending under-resourced schools across South and East Los Angeles was not simply about fostering positive youth development in a neutral, context-free way; instead, it was about fostering empowering youth development within a particular social and political context.

Shawn Ginwright and Julio Cammarota (2002) criticize positive youth development theory precisely because of its inattention to the social and political contexts within which urban youth are developing; as they argue, "A discussion of these forces is particularly important for youth who struggle with issues of identity, racism, sexism, police brutality, and poverty that are supported by unjust economic policies" (p. 82). Furthermore, they propose that positive youth development theory does not position adolescents as active participants in defining their identities and negotiating opportunities for their maturation. They instead call for a model of social justice youth development, a framework that "accounts for the multiple forms of oppression youth encounter and highlights the strategies they use to address inequities plaguing their communities" (p. 83).

YPAR fits perfectly into this social justice development model as a strategy to help young people address these inequities. A concern with helping young people understand and then act upon their social and political environment has led us to focus not only on students' academic identity development, but their civic identity development as well. While scholars have developed different terms to capture this aspect of identity related to public engagement—including socio-historical identity, socio-political identity, and political-moral identity, to name a few—the umbrella term, "civic identity," generally refers to one's understanding of and relation to a particular community or polity, as well as one's sense of agency to act within it (Youniss, McLelland, & Yates, 1997).

While it may seem at first that status as a citizen is either something that you have or do not have, a growing number of scholars are rejecting the idea that citizenship is a static, standardized entity that everyone experiences in the same way and are seeking to recast civic identity in a way that privileges the experiences of low-income students and students of color (Banks, 2008; Lawy & Biesta, 2007; Nasir & Kirshner, 2003). These theorists draw directly from socio-cultural theories of learning and identity to highlight the shifting, practice-based nature of civic identity. Watts & Flanagan (2007) offer a model of civic identity development that emphasizes liberation and empowerment; they argue that traditional notions of political socialization "implicitly encourage investment in or identi-fication with the prevailing social order and replication of it," and ask, "Are young members of marginalized groups as likely as more socially integrated youth to replicate or buy into a system where they feel excluded?" (p. 781). Their model of civic (what they call socio-political) identity development centers on a critical rather than normative understanding of the systemic forces shaping society that validates the experiences of young people of color and offers them avenues for developing liberating political efficacy.

The team knew that as they introduced students to the Council, they were going to be asking these young people to grapple with information about inequality in society that was not only complex and difficult to grasp on an intellectual level, but deeply relevant and sometimes painful for them in terms of what they were experiencing in their families and communities as their civic identities developed. Consider the concept of social reproduction—the idea that inequality replicates itself generation after generation through a combination of social structures and individual behaviors. Without appropriate support and critical analysis, young people struggling with poverty who learn about social reproduction could take a negative view of their own communities and lose hope about the possibilities of growth and transformation.

As a result, the adults found it crucial to build relationships of caring and trust with young people so that they could discuss these provocative issues openly and encourage them to work through the emotions that would inevitably arise as they tested out their civic agency in a society that often attempted to marginalize their voices. In *Subtractive Schooling: U.S.–Mexican Youth and the Politics of Caring*, Angela Valenzuela (1999) argued that traditional schooling structures often ignore the context in which students are living and the funds of knowledge that they bring to education by focusing narrowly on academic learning, testing, and accountability; as a result, education can be "culturally subtractive," leaving students feeling invisible or marginalized. The Council operates instead from Valenzuela's concept of "culturally additive" education—one that is not afraid to re-introduce the concepts of caring and love to teaching and learning and strives to make students feel supported so that they can achieve to their highest potential.

In her foundational work on caring, Nel Noddings (1984) argues that the typical logic of schooling does not permit the kind of extended contact between teachers and students that is needed to build strong relationships. Teachers often see multiple groups of students over the course of a school day in 45- to 90-minute chunks several times per week, moving on to new students from school year to school year. The Council—and particularly the Summer Seminar—brought teach-ers and students into contact for over eight hours per day over five weeks, during which time they not only worked on a high-interest and meaningful project, but ate and laughed and drove around the city together. This model allowed the students to get to know each other and the teachers on a deeper level, fostering bonds that led students to refer to the Council as a "family."

These familial bonds permitted the deep exploration of inequitable schooling conditions to be an empowering rather than discouraging activity. Importantly, the teachers who led the Council teams thought carefully about which students would benefit most from being invited into this family, which will be explored in the next section.

Recruiting and Incentivizing Students

Considering the level of commitment that the Council asked its members to give to the program and the amount of resources invested into every Council student, the group required students to fill out an application to join the 2010 Summer Seminar. Unlike many summer enrichment programs, however, the Council did not determine eligibility based on academic indicators; in fact, the application stated explicitly, "There is *no* grade point average requirement to participate in Summer Seminar."

Instead, the application offered information about what students would be signing up for; namely, "to study the various social, economic, cultural, and political factors that impact their schooling and their trajectories toward college." Applicants were asked to give a two-year commitment to the Council that, since teachers largely recruited rising juniors, would ensure that students would remain with the group through their high school graduation.

The teachers varied in how they went about identifying students who would be a strong fit for the program. Most took to heart the idea of offering this opportunity to students who displayed unrealized potential that could be coaxed out in the unique Council learning environment. Fred described the students he would encourage to join:

> I chose those folks that were kind of on the fence—you could see the potential, you could see their want to learn. They asked really great questions, but they weren't academically savvy. But they just inherently had this little fire in them that I felt like, if there was some structure, if there was some guidance, if we throw some good stuff their way, they would be powerful students.

Veronica took a similar approach, explaining how she sought out the students who were "on the edge of thinking that school sucks, but were also very creative and talented." Based on her understanding of the Council's critical learning model, she liked to take on students who other teachers thought couldn't learn and who "needed a different kind of environment to develop their skills and channel that energy into something really positive."

The recruitment process could differ for teachers whose involvement in the Council was just beginning. Since the 2010 seminar was Eddie's first, he found himself drawn to students with whom he already had built relationships and could trust to commit to the program; as he explained, "three of four of them were actually very stellar academic students." Eddie saw the value in bringing academically successful students into the fold not only for their own development, but for his as well. "I always say I was blessed with having this group in helping me through this process," he said, "because it was a learning process for them doing this YPAR work just as much as it was for me. They just made a good fit because they kind of allowed me to grow with them through this process." This reflection serves as a reminder of the critical pedagogy that guided the Council—the students could serve as guides and the teachers could lean on them for support.

Importantly, while the teachers went about encouraging students to join the Council based on complex ideas about learning styles and student empowerment, the students themselves often described choosing to join for different reasons— ones based on the classic adolescent desires for friendship and belonging (and food). As Miguel explained, "I actually learned about the Council through two of my good friends, Greg and Elizabeth. I was looking for something to join, and they told me there was food, so I went. And I saw that the teacher leading it was Mr. Tan, so I decided to check it out."

Some students did possess a developing critical consciousness that drove their participation; as Karina shared, "I think I joined because I felt that not everyone got the same amount of resources in school, so I wanted to see why everything happened and how I could help that. I like talking to different students, I like learning about the different communities." Indeed, many of the students drawn to the program had outgoing and gregarious personalities and were not too afraid to build friendships with students they had never met before from schools around the city.

While the Council was committed to offering students transformational learning experiences, it also manifested its commitment to youth development by ensuring that students would receive concrete benefits for participation. Ernest and John worked with the UCLA Graduate School of Education to offer college credit to students who completed the Summer Seminar; in addition, a partnership with the City of Los Angeles summer jobs program allowed the students to be hired as researchers and receive a small salary for their work. Since many of the Council students found themselves confronted with the dilemma each summer of whether to invest in their education or work to support themselves and their families, offering these incentives was an important way to tell students that their time and effort was valued and that their full investment in the program would be worthwhile.

Icebreakers and Relationship-Building

Much of the relationship-building that took place early in the summer seminar involved fun, ice-breaker activities to get students talking across schools and beginning to feel comfortable with each other and their researcher identities. For instance, the first day of the 2010 Summer Seminar began with a Human Bingo game in which the students had to race around the room finding other students who met different criteria on the board the adults had created—students who were, for instance, the youngest children in their families, or the biggest Dodgers fans, or experts at dance moves that they would be willing to share with the group.

The game included several items that subtly hinted at students' civic identities; for example, students were asked to find others who had been involved in a protest, or who had interviewed a public official. But overall, this was an opportunity for students to have some fun and meet each other. Students could not claim Bingo unless the names they filled in on their board were from schools that they themselves did not attend, and the process of reviewing the responses helped everyone begin to learn names and personalities.

The first day of the seminar also featured a photo scavenger hunt of the UCLA campus, which took place in mixed school teams so that students could get to know each other and the various adults in the group. For many of the students, the seminar was the first opportunity they had to spend an extended amount of time on a college campus, and the adults found it important to take advantage of UCLA to expose students to information about post-secondary education and undergraduate life in general. This concern with college access led the team to dedicate an entire morning during the first week of the seminar to providing students with information about the college application process as well as an entire afternoon to a personal statement workshop to give students a jump-start.

While these activities were not strictly related to the YPAR endeavor, they were crucial to the endeavor of investing in the lives of the Council students. More important than the results of the research projects were the academic, social/emotional, and civic benefits that the team sought to provide to the students who became part of the Council family. And as the adults shared and read excerpts of the college personal statements that the students wrote, the relationships grew stronger. Consider the trust and strength of character that Gustavo exhibited through his writing:

> *I come from a family that has ups and downs, but they never give up until they achieve what they want to accomplish. Living in a huge community where there are few opportunities, it is difficult to find success. In South Central, where violence and suffering rules, it is very difficult for people to better their education because they are constantly bombarded with problems in school or at home. In spite of this, I always look up to my big sister because of her success—coming from an uneducated family, she is in college and has succeeded, which makes me admire her. She is the one who keeps motivating me to continue forward in going to college. Being part of a family that is very united, I would love to succeed and make my parents proud and show everyone that no matter how many obstacles I go through, anything is possible.*

Moving into YPAR

Embedded into the relationship-building that consumed much of the first week of the summer seminar were brief forays into social theory and data about educational and social inequities that would serve as the foundation for the research that would guide the Council's work from that point forward.

As students filtered into the Law School classroom on the second day of the seminar, they saw a map of Los Angeles projected onto the screen on the front wall. The city was displayed in a spectrum of color, from bright white to dark black with various shades of gray in between. Ernest asked students to put their names on post-its, walk up to the screen, and place the post-its on the part of the city in which they lived. Within a few minutes, groups of yellow post-its clustered around the neighborhoods of South and East Los Angeles—neighborhoods that were colored black on the map. Ernest then placed a post-it on the screen to represent UCLA's location. He then revealed that the map was a graphic representation of racial and economic segregation and inequality in the city.

Students reflected on the dividing lines—the concentrations of wealth and pockets of extreme poverty—and considered where their homes and schools were located. These reflections segued into a reading about social reproduction that attempted to answer some of the students' questions about why inequality seemed so intractable over generations. While the conversation shifted back toward college personal statements later in the day, discussions of inequality returned the next day with an exploration of strategies for challenging inequality. Freire's ideas about critical pedagogy played a starring role.

The interplay between forging familial bonds and introducing challenging and complex social issues was consciously and meticulously planned in order to provide the support and trust needed for students to embark upon an educational journey that could be painful at times, but was largely characterized by hope and agency.

Moving Forward

As these chapters proceed and we detail the research process that the Council engaged in during the 2010–2011 school year, it will be impossible to extricate the relationship-building elements of the work from the research elements since they happened simultaneously and symbiotically. The transformation of the small research teams into tight working groups was a necessary precondition for creating research questions, collecting data in the field, and developing sophisticated presentations. The relationship building took place constantly and informally—during lunches on the UCLA campus, during the breaks from the grueling process of transcribing and coding data, and during the car rides with teachers to and from various interview sites.

Nonetheless, we felt it crucial to begin with an exploration of this pedagogy of relationships in order to emphasize that YPAR cannot succeed without it. As much planning must go into the careful crafting of a community of practice as the development of a research theme. Now, on to the research.

References

Banks, J. A. (2008). Diversity, group identity, and citizenship education in a global age. *Educational Researcher, 37*(3), 129–139.

Bryk, A., & Schneider, B. (2004). *Trust in schools: A core resource for improvement.* New York: Russell Sage Foundation.

Ginwright, S., & Cammarota, J. (2002). New terrain in youth development: The promise of a social justice approach. *Social Justice, 29*(4), 82–95.

Larson, R. (2000). Toward a psychology of positive youth development. *American Psychologist, 55*(1), 170–183.

Lave, J., & Wenger, E. (1991). *Situated learning: Legitimate peripheral participation.* Cambridge: Cambridge University Press.

Lawy, R., & Biesta, G. (2007). Citizenship-as-practice: The educational implications of an inclusive and relational understanding of citizenship. *British Journal of Educational Studies, 54*(1), 34–50.

Nasir, N., & Kirshner, B. (2003). The cultural construction of moral and civic identities. *Applied Developmental Science, 7*, 138–147.

Noddings, N. (1984). *Caring: A feminine approach to ethics and moral education.* Berkeley: University of California Press.

Rogoff, B. (2003). *The cultural nature of human development.* New York: Oxford University Press.

Valenzuela, A. (1999). *Subtractive schooling: U.S.–Mexican youth and the politics of caring.* New York: SUNY Press.

Vygotsky, L. (1978). *Mind in society.* Cambridge: Harvard University Press.

Watts, R., & Flanagan, C. (2007). Pushing the envelope on civic engagement: A developmental and liberation psychology perspective. *The Journal of Community Psychology, 35*, 779–792.

Youniss, J., McLellan, J., & Yates, M. (1997). What we know about engendering civic identity. *American Behavioral Scientist, 40*(5), 620–631.

FIGURE 4 Council students from Roosevelt High School present at the UCLA Labor Center in Los Angeles

FIGURE 5 Council students from Crenshaw High School deconstruct critical social theory in their presentation

INTERLUDE

Brokering Relationships in the Council

In this conversation, Nicole and Antero talk with three educators—Mark Bautista, Ebony Cain, and Antonio Martinez—who worked with the Council as UCLA graduate students during the 2010–2011 school year. The discussion highlights the importance of building trust with students before engaging them in the vulnerable work of critical research, as well as the ways that this process transforms the identities of the adults involved.

Nicole: We all played multiple roles within this community. How do you feel about the way your roles developed over time?

Antonio: Thinking back on my experience, I was fortunate to work with a teacher who had been with the Council for a good number of years and had a strong understanding about what some of its foundation and principles were. I do remember that when I first started working with him, I was surprised when he told me that the previous graduate researcher had brought food and candy to the group so maybe that's what my role should be, too. [laughs] I think I had a reaction to that expectation initially, but over time I began to see that at about 4:30 p.m. *all* of us started to get hungry, right? And we needed that extra energy boost to do that work that was going on into the later hours of the evening and a lot of times into the night. And so I thought okay—we need food, we all get hungry and I can get some food. You know what? I'm the one with the flexible schedule so it makes a lot of sense that I'm the one doing that kind of work.

        Over time, I began to see that it was also important for me to think about how I was *performing* as a researcher. And it really drew from my background as a performing arts teacher—I was trying to tap into some of my own experiences working with young people in that way where we can also bring out this side of them that is really authentic to their voice and really speaks to an audience. That was something I hadn't anticipated, either. In terms of instruction, I think that in our space it was very different because sometimes we would use more of an organic curriculum than the more structured conversations we'd have as graduate students.

Mark: Building on that idea of organic pedagogy that Antonio was talking about, I remember when I first got into the Council and I asked the teacher that Antonio was talking about if he came up with a lesson plan. I remember him saying, "What lesson plan? This is straight from the dome—you gotta come organic." From that day on I learned how much of an organic pedagogue this teacher was and how much of an organic pedagogue I wasn't. So whenever it came to working with the students, my two main roles were to, one: always come with the lesson plan, and two: always be prepared for something different, because that was the only way we were going to keep the attention of the students. And my second role was actually bringing food as well because that was a big part of our pedagogy. My mom and my mother-in-law and my wife would actually make food for our students because we always knew that without that sustenance that they needed after school they weren't going to engage at all. So I think that became my role throughout the years.

Antero: I'm curious if you ever got directives from Ernest or John saying, "This is what your role is. This is what you need to do." How did you know what was expected of you as a graduate student?

Ebony: I think one of the important pieces of the Council is that apprenticeship model that we often talk about. So, just to speak to Ernest's role in the process of teaching and learning, he and John and Nicole did a certain amount of modeling about what to expect from the teachers and the students. Some of the informal, cultural things that were modeled were things like being on time, being prepared, and thinking about how we related to each other and how the students were expected to relate to each other. And there wouldn't have to be any explicit conversation about these things. That was how this space was different from your traditional academic space. There were some conversations happening informally. When the adults arrived to Council meetings, they would pull out their computers and start writing and reflecting. The students would come in, see that, and start following those same behaviors.

Nicole: What's the balance between someone telling you what to do in an educational space and learning by doing through the apprenticeship model?

Mark: We definitely used an apprenticeship model in which the students would look at and kind of mimic their adult peers. But at the same time, it was an apprenticeship model for the graduate student researchers to look at what John Rogers and Ernest Morrell were doing as professionals. To look at Nicole and how she ran the program, and to look at how dope all the other teachers were. And I think over time you just take bits and pieces of everybody's pedagogy and you create your own. But then at the same time I think what is really important is looking toward your students as role models as well and learning from them. Because I think the learning process wasn't just for the students to learn to do research but was also for us as graduate student researchers and critical educators to learn about the experiences of these students and to really figure out how to take action. How do we analyze our own experiences? What can we learn from our students' experiences to get better at the jobs that we do? There really wasn't any job description that anybody tells you—you just kind of figure it out along the way.

Antonio: Yeah, I'm glad you brought that up, Mark, because as far as action, I think that's exactly it. I was the youngest of all of us and so what that means is you all graduated before me and as you all left I realized I was becoming the more senior representative—if that's even possible—as far as the Council is concerned. I really felt that urgency to think about how I step up. It was really pushing me to try new things out.

Nicole: Over and over again we hear this theme that there is something special about teaching and learning in the Council versus what it means to teach and learn in school spaces. I know that many of us have come from teaching backgrounds and I wonder if you could reflect on what it is that makes the Council so different from what it feels like in a traditional classroom. I would even extend that since a lot of us are in academia now. What is different about being a researcher in the Council?

Ebony: I think one of the things that comes up right away is what I call "carpool pedagogy." All of us were driving students home. We were driving students to presentations. And in the car, waiting for people to get in and out, that's when the real conversations happened. That's where the application of this theory and the life-changing moments really happened—in those non-traditional spaces. We had the opportunity to really develop relationships and come from a place of trust and honor each other as individuals as part of our community: "You are an important part of my community—so much so that I'm going to drive you one hour to the Valley to go home and you aren't going to call your parents and tell them to get you." And it was always the craziest thing—students sharing their music and me sharing mine. That is when the work happens. That is when the real critical conversations took place that we then got to bring back to the formal learning spaces in the conference room or in the presentation. That's one of those things that might not exist in traditional academic settings but that really does enhance and deepen those skills and benefits participants of this program and the community.

Antonio: I think that what was really important around the Council in terms of this different model of teaching and learning is that it went both ways—it applied to both the young people and the adults in the room. For us it was really about taking the time to sit and talk with students. It took me a while to really catch on that this was a pedagogical component of the work we were doing. Sometimes I would think about the timing of YPAR and that we needed to start researching and we needed to take action, but it was really important to stop and take the time to hear young people and the high points of their week and maybe some things that they were struggling with. When you think about it, when do young people really have a chance to sit and listen and talk with each other? I think that was one of the biggest aspects of our space in South Los Angeles; it allowed young people to see the humanity of the other young people that were in that room. It really made me think about what I was going to share in that circle, and it was a place for me to be as genuine as I could with them.

Mark: I think the non-traditional learning process is that you would have to show up. What I mean by show up is be honest with one another and speak from your own experiences and truths. Only when you were able to show up could you ever expect the students to show up. I saw the power of this type of educational space and pedagogy when we would be in the hotel working with our students at one or two in the morning, practicing their presentations for the next day. And you could see the students exhausted and the teachers exhausted and still they're in the same space trying to perfect their skills at being presenters of this research and speaking from their own experiences. When I would have those moments with students, I felt like this was a real learning process. We all understood that this work matters. I think that is what made this space so empowering.

Nicole: I remember those nights. Those were some of the most powerful times.

Antonio: The relationships that we build with young people really extend beyond our after-school hours. There were many times we had to work on the weekends. They're at our house, we're cooking dinner, we're doing whatever we need to do to support ourselves in the process. And I'm saying all that because it's hard. It feels like the lines of our roles as graduate student researchers really blur. We're involved with them in this YPAR program and as supporters in their school day and we're also working with their teachers who are also coming to these meetings and staying up with us until 2 or 3 in the morning.

FIGURE 6 Council students from Locke High School present their research about powerful leadership

4

ASKING RESEARCH QUESTIONS

WRITING PROMPT #3
JULY 9, 2010

Yosso's article describes the community cultural wealth of People of Color. This wealth includes knowledge, skills, abilities, family, language, and social contacts. Describe the community cultural wealth in your community and explain how this could be brought into your school.

My community has always been overlooked but what they don't know is that it's not a bad community. They say that they are all lazy, that all they do is stay home. Most of my neighbors work but some stay home to take care of their little children.

My community is mostly known for all the shooting and incidents that happens. Most people have families that have graduated from high school and have good decent jobs. Most of the people in my community are African-American but they still understand Spanish. Most of the Hispanics in my community try their best to understand and talk English. We all get along as if we are family. In my community we try our best to make it clean. We clean the sidewalk and other things. We all help each other out when we need something. It is a nice community because most of the people don't stereotype each other like they do in other communities.

It could be brought to school by us because we show how we are and they think that that's how our community is. That the students don't respect their teachers that they also just go because their friends go to school. Most of the teachers get mad and start saying whatever comes to their minds. It can also be brought to our school by starting a program or something that talks about the communities and they could go look around the communities and see what they find. The abilities that the communities might have are that they could help anyone that needs help.

Angelica, 11th grader

In Yosso's article she talks about the community cultural wealth of people of color meaning the knowledge, skills, abilities, family language, and social contacts in the community.

The community cultural wealth in my community is mostly unsuccessful but those who succeed motivate others to continue dreaming and believing in themselves that they can be someone important in life. For example when I was in 9th grade my friends didn't really care about school, their only goal was to graduate high school and now their goal is to graduate high school and at least graduate from community college.

What makes my community think that way is that they mostly come from African American or Latino families which are low income families that have not attend college meaning they will be the 1st person in their family going to college. Yet there are some students that because nobody in their family has been to college are more motivated to be the 1st ones and make their family proud. There are also students that are not motivated or even think of going to college because of their friends. On the other hand there are students that are very motivated to go to college because of family, friends or programs.

Crenshaw should bring into my school, my community social wealth by having more programs involved with us like the Council because it changes students for good and motivates them that people of color can make a difference and go to college.

Bernardo, 11th grader

Angelica and Bernardo brought their personal experiences to bear as they wrestled with complex social theories. While people often think that asking a research question represents the beginning of a research project, we have found that the questions typically emerge later in YPAR projects only after relational trust is built and students connect what they viscerally know from their own lived experience with literature in the field that gives new language to those experiences. While this chapter will describe how Council students, teachers, and researchers worked together to develop research questions informed by critical theory that guided their subsequent data collection and analysis, we want to begin by first acknowledging the process of intellectual growth and development that sets the stage for these provocative questions to develop. We will explore how students engaged with dense philosophical texts and detail the iterative learning processes that moved students to the point where they could design actionable questions to guide their YPAR inquiry.

Tackling Critical Social Theory

As part of the Council's model of critical praxis, students produced and shared daily reflections in response to adult-written writing prompts. The prompts encouraged synthesis of the topics and theories being shared. As seen in the two reflections above, the prompts encouraged an engagement with academic texts like Tara Yosso's (2005) article "Whose culture has capital? A critical race theory discussion of community cultural wealth." Students received a copy of this article as part of a seminar course reader that the adults had printed through UCLA each year. The reader mirrored the ones that undergraduates and graduate students pay for in university classes and represented an important component for supporting academic and college readiness through the Council.

The reflection above was the third that students had completed in the summer seminar, and the second one that had students responding directly to theory. The previous prompt had students grappling with Freirean explanations of a *banking* model of education. Angelica and Bernardo's responses to this question about the assets of their communities highlights that Yosso's expansion of "wealth" encourages various points of entry and opportunity for personal engagement. Yosso delineates six different forms of cultural "wealth" in her article, including: Aspirational, Linguistic, Familial, Social, Navigational, and Resistant Capital (pp. 77–80).

Yosso outlined these forms of community cultural wealth as part of a movement to "restructure U.S. social institutions around those knowledges, skills, abilities and networks—the community cultural wealth—possessed and utilized by People of Color" (p. 82). Grounded in the ideas of Critical Race Theory (Crenshaw, 2002; Matsuda 1991), Yosso's work speaks to the networked "funds of knowledge" (Moll, Amanti, Neff, & Gonzalez, 1992) members of the Council bring with them into their seminar space. The placement of this text early on in the seminar was a deliberate one: though challenging, Yosso's work both validated the knowledges and skills students possessed and established the kind of academic rigor expected from students in the program.

Helping young people understand a complex concept like cultural capital is a difficult task. Texts like Yosso's are typically relegated to graduate-level coursework, and the challenge taken up by the Council adults was to unpack complex research in ways that resonated with high school students without watering down the intellectual concepts at hand. The adults did not assign a text like Yosso's for homework and expect students to come back with the same level of understanding as a Ph.D. student might. Further, they did not always ask students to read every word of the voluminous amount of research provided in the course reader, instead demonstrating reading and annotating strategies that students could use to tackle challenging articles and gain meaning about the main ideas. Considering that many of the students needed academic supports and were classified in their schools as struggling, "dependent" readers (Beers, 2002), the Council adults sought to show students how to highlight, question, and use the margins in the course reader to process their thinking. The practices that the group engaged in around the course reader represented one of the ways that YPAR pursued critical, personal, and academic purposes simultaneously.

Literacy development within the Council was based on the belief that analysis of complex texts must be grounded in the familiar contexts of student lives and interests; hence, the explicit focus on unpacking academic language and asking students to reflect on connections they could make to the text. The abstract language and passive voice characteristic of much academic writing justly gives critical theory a reputation of being difficult to read; however, when theory is presented in the context of lived experience and time is taken to unpack a clunkily translated or particularly dense paragraph, we found that students were able to move fluidly toward a strong understanding of critical theory.

While certain authors, including Freire and Yosso, were constants from year to year in the Council in order to ground students in critical understandings of education research, policy, and practice, other articles came and went as needed to highlight specific themes that applied to particular research topics. During the 2010 summer seminar, readings in critical social theory were supplemented with articles particularly relevant to the *Williams v. California* court case. (See Appendix B for the entire summer seminar 2010 reading list.)

Every choice that adults made in the construction of the course reader was intentional, even down to including the full citations for all articles. Students were encouraged to refer to key texts by authors' last names and publication years in order to socialize them into the practices of adult researchers. We note the full citations here, as they, too, presented a learning experience within the Council. Having students *see* the way that citations were formatted according to the style of the American Psychological Association gave them access to the hidden curriculum of academic scholarship that is often glossed over in secondary classroom settings. The teachers made sure that the readers were bound in the exact format of a college reader and required students to bring them to the seminar each day, illustrating the seriousness with which they expected students to take their scholarship.

While adults led discussions, organized group work, and offered brief lectures to help students build understanding of these graduate-level texts, they took pains to reassure students that they did not need to believe in the viewpoints the authors expressed. As the reflections that open this chapter highlight, students often absorbed theory from the summer seminar while interpreting the world around them in very different ways.

Angelica and Bernardo's contrasting viewpoints demonstrate the different directions that students took with the readings. Angelica's use of the "we" pronoun feels much different from Bernardo's use of "they" to describe community members, indicating varying levels of connection to communities. When Angelica uses "they," she is referring to outsiders looking in upon her community. She offers her perspective on how outsiders think about where she lives: a space with "lazy" individuals, "shooting incidents," and disrespectful students. Claim by claim, she challenges these assumptions, doing so while also articulating the cultural wealth that is so valued within her community. And near the end of her reflection, she plants the seeds of understanding how research could represent a way of taking action to present counter-stories to challenge dominant narratives. She writes, "It [community cultural wealth] can also be brought to our school by starting a program or something that talks about the communities and they could go look around the communities and see what they find." Angelica predicted the process she was about to engage in through her words.

Bernardo also seeks similar programs like the Council to highlight community cultural wealth in his school. He shares Angelica's sentiments about the assumptions made by others about his community but also implicitly endorses some of these assumptions by suggesting that efforts made by his community to fight stereotypes are "mostly unsuccessful." Bernardo's reflection suggested the various perspectives that students brought to the Council.

And so what happened after students wrote these reflections? Rather than simply being tucked away as completed assignments, the reflections helped formalize pathways toward research. They became artifacts just as important as the peer-reviewed article by Yosso in informing the questions that students were gearing up to ask about their communities. Council adults, by treating student writing as legitimate spaces for exploration and learning, mentored students to become active researchers and media producers. Discussions about the intersection of theoretical texts and student experiences became key steps in the cycle of iterative inquiry in the Council.

Iteration of Research Questions

Asking research questions is an iterative process. It is an intellectual journey that begins with individual experiences, coalesces within one's community of practice, and is refined with the introduction of new perspectives and theories. In keeping with the ideas of sociocultural learning theory, research questions are culturally mediated and change as the researcher's understanding of society also changes and becomes more nuanced.

As detailed in the previous chapter, YPAR is built on several key relational and pedagogical components coming together. First, youth, teachers, and university researchers must come together around a unified purpose geared toward taking action in space that fosters trust and comfort. These two components— mutual acknowledgment of a common purpose and a shared respect for each other's viewpoints—are the foundation on which any YPAR endeavor must be built. Though there is perhaps an idyllic vision of YPAR groups simply emerging organically without much planning, we have found intentionality to be key when establishing a place for YPAR. The development of and engagement with one's "critical consciousness" (Freire, 1970) is a key prerequisite to engaging in the research process. The icebreakers that comprised much of the first week of the summer seminar were carefully developed to include activities aimed at helping the participants look critically at the world around them and learn from and with each other. Activities like the college campus scavenger hunt, noted in the last chapter, allowed members of the Council to get to know each other, share in social life at UCLA, and gain experience in higher education settings. The parallel development of interpersonal, critical, and academic understandings was key to the process.

Clearly, developing research questions was not a straightforward process, but one that included starts and stops and circular journeys of discovery. YPAR requires comfort with the folding in of theory, experience, and uncertainty as part of a complex inquiry process that begins long before students and teachers set foot on the university campus.

The Cycle of Inquiry

Once students and teachers feel comfortable talking about social and educational equity in a community of practice filled with safety and trust, how do youth actually begin the process of developing the complex research questions that will guide their work for the rest of the school year? Just as the process of understanding social theory is a cyclical one involving movement between personal experience and outside knowledge, so is the process of deciding upon a final research question. The continuous development of new insights brought about by listening to peers, reading articles, and reflecting on long-held beliefs makes gleaning the exact origins of the Council's research questions difficult. While students come to the seminar with some hypotheses about their communities and why certain conditions exist that lead them toward particular questions, their thinking evolves by reflecting on something like Yosso's theory of community cultural wealth, leading them down new paths of inquiry. Once they think they've settled on a question again, another reading makes them rethink their entire framework.

Considering the limited sense of research engagement with which students begin the seminar, their thinking about research questions takes huge leaps and bounds when they first engage with new ideas. They vacillate wildly between questions as they sort through exhilarating new ideas. This process is refined over time as students integrate new ideas into their theoretical frameworks and move closer to deciding upon a researchable question. (See Figure 4.1 for a visual representation of this process.)

Though knowledge about a topic is initially limited (indicating a smaller range in topics for research), this space for learning balloons with engagement with theory over time. As understanding of these theories is refined, students may narrow their questions again into something that can be fruitfully explored over the course of a summer or a school year. For instance, at the beginning of the seminar, students were encouraged to consider overarching questions, such as "What is an adequate education?" and "What does every student deserve from schools in California?" Over time, these questions were filtered through the sociocultural lenses of theory and reflection. The final research questions, shared later in this chapter, highlight how such broad questions lend themselves toward empirical

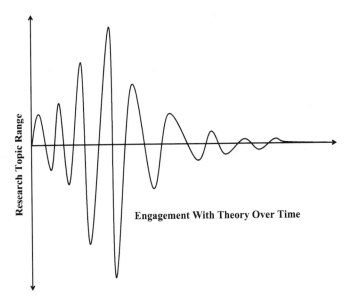

FIGURE 4.1 Process of Developing Research Questions

research when narrowed down to manageable chunks. The process of developing research questions follows a typical trajectory that broadens widely in scope until existing research, analysis, and hypotheses narrow the focus. Even over time, the specific nuances of a question may be adjusted, but they move toward a limit.

The chicken and the egg question about whether to start the research process with theories or questions thus becomes meaningless in the YPAR framework; designing YPAR research questions is a constant cycle of questioning and theory building leading toward a nuanced topic that can be empirically explored within a limited amount of time with available resources. The power of the Council's work to get to the heart of issues of inequality derived from the ways theory and personal experiences were so finely ingrained in the pith of academic research from the start of the research process.

Moving beyond a "Problem"

Of course, this isn't to say that research comes from a singular lived experience. As Angelica and Bernardo's opening vignettes suggest, students take up theory and their understanding of the world in very different ways. In fact, we shared Bernardo's reflection here because his was a viewpoint frequently shared at the beginning of the summer seminar. When Bernardo wrote, "There are also students that are not motivated or even think of going to college because of their friends," he highlighted a common tendency we saw among young people over the years when they first joined the Council to place blame for the "problems" in education on themselves and their own communities. Analyzing data about educational inequity, particularly decades-long challenges in large urban school systems like the one in Los Angeles, initially highlights to students that, among the constant flux of policy, school structures, and facilities, the only real constant in education is the youth themselves. Perhaps, they think, the students and their social experiences are the problem.

As with much of the rest of the model of the summer seminar, this too is an important space in which personal understandings brush shoulders with educational theory—a space for adult researchers to give students language to understand how their life experiences align with the decades of critical research. Student experiences have been sullied by "bad teaching"? We call that the "banking model of education" as explained by Paulo Freire (1970). Students are not motivated and act out in classrooms? That's frequently called an "oppositional identity" (Ogbu, 1995). In unpacking student reflections and coming up with research questions, the Council helped students develop a common, theory-instantiated vocabulary to name inequity in schools and to reconcile different interpretations of lived experiences.

The critical consciousness supported in the summer seminar allowed students and teachers alike to "perceive the reality of oppression not as a closed world from which there is no exit, but as a limiting situation which they can transform" (Freire, 1970, p. 34). When examining legacies of inequality, young people's immediate reactions might be to see themselves and the problems of schools through a deficit lens. Critical research can provide a different framework in which to understand these legacies and in the process foment in students a productive "political anger" (Ruitenberg, 2009). The vocabulary of contextualized theory allows students to see that just because something is not right in schools does not mean that they or their communities are "wrong."

Rather than positioning students as merely objects who experience inequality in schools, the process of accessing research and forming research questions makes a positional shift toward viewing students as subjects of transformative change. By being able to *name* the questions and the aspects of inequality to be challenged through research, students take a stronger ownership in changing and addressing the many forms of inequality they have experienced in schools. Too often, research and teacher education programs address the "problems" of urban communities. In her reflection on working with pre-service teachers, Marcelle Haddix discusses the assumptions many of her often-white preservice teachers make about expecting to enter and "help" communities of people of color, without fully looking at the forms of cultural wealth present in these spaces. Similarly, the problematic lumping-in of many different, diverse spaces as a singular, monolithic "community" is also troublesome (Philip, Way, Garcia, Schuler-Brown, & Navarro, 2013). By recognizing these tensions, YPAR allows students to consider the issues facing their communities from their first-hand perspectives from a position of belonging and love and with the purpose of creating sustained and welcome change.

Ultimately, YPAR pushes students and the broader educational research community to challenge the notion of the *problem* of urban schools. By researching the existing inequities, students build on powerful, organic histories of resistance and cultural wealth. An expansion of critical consciousness allows members of the Council to ask questions instead of making assumptions about deficits in their communities. It is at this point that they become ready to take up the specific topics selected for the summer seminar.

As explained in the previous chapter, students devised their research questions within a framework developed by the adults in the group. Ernest and John selected the 10-year anniversary of the filing of the *Williams v. California* case as the theme for the 2010 seminar. Teachers then pinpointed the specific topics they would take on: teaching, resources, leadership, social/physical ecology, and curriculum. Within these five areas of inquiry, students were able to find their own connections to how the research topic affected them along multiple points of intersection in their educational, social, and cultural lives.

As students and teachers developed research questions, the adult researchers advised them just as they would their doctoral students preparing their dissertation studies. In particular, there were two key considerations that the students were asked to consider. First, is the question being asked one that has not been answered yet? Second, can this question be empirically answered within the school year?

In terms of the first question, students had no problem finding entry points where they could offer previously unheard perspectives on conditions of inequality in schools considering the exclusion of youth voices from most academic literature. They built upon preliminary data about the effects of the Williams Settlement and upon their own experiences to set the tone for the questions they investigated. The more difficult proposition was to ensure that the questions students asked were researchable—not too broad and not too narrow. The adult researchers played a key role in helping guide how students' questions were worded and framed within the larger Council framework.

Research for What?

Concurrent to working on the development of specific research questions, Council students were also pushed to think about the rationale for their research during the summer seminar. Just as graduate students must propose a thesis or dissertation prior to undertaking research, students were required to present their draft questions internally to their peers and the other adults to gather feedback and suggestions before moving forward with their research. In a sense, the culminating presentations that emerged five weeks later represented "defenses" for students' research and a means for the Council to celebrate the hard work that was undertaken over a five-week period.

Part of the process of developing research questions involved guiding students to understand the difference between a *topic* they were investigating—"the general problem/issue that your research will address"—and a research *question*—"something that can be researched about the topic and hopefully answered." Nicole presented these definitions to students during a workshop dedicated to crafting research questions. As groups developed questions, they presented them to Ernest, Nicole, and the other graduate students for feedback. Questions that could be answered with a simple yes/no, questions too broad or narrow in scope, questions that reflected student biases: all were sent back to the proverbial drawing board for revision.

Further, the summer seminar was designed for students to consider how their research could lead to actionable outcomes. Students and teachers examined community resources, possible venues for sharing findings down the road, and methodologies that would likely yield responses from policy makers and local stakeholders to make sure that they got the most bang for their buck in the questions they chose to explore. In addition to informing academic and local communities, the Council research was framed as a means to instantiate change within schools among both policies and practices.

Students and teachers made these strategic choices to pose research questions that could grab the attention of administrators and policy makers because they believed in a common purpose for this research grounded in the idea of acting upon the world and empowering community members to be involved in the struggle for justice. This was not simply doing research for the sake of an academic exercise—it was a political act staking a claim for the right of young people to speak their truth to power and demand change.

While the following chapter will focus on the methodologies the students employed to collect data about their research questions, it is important here to note that we framed the knowledge and lived experiences that students brought to the Council as valid data to be mined and shared as part of this process. Within research communities, the honoring of youth experiences is a key value that is often overlooked or simply assumed to be present without much interrogation or reflection. YPAR encourages researchers to reflect on young people not simply as members of an undifferentiated mass of "students," but as complex individuals with brilliant insights to provide about themselves, their schools, and their society.

Developing Research Questions

If the process of understanding a research issue is an iterative one that constantly tightens in scope, as explored in Figure 4.1, at what point do we finally move forward with the research questions that youth and teachers develop in cohorts over the summer? This question, too, can be explained by illuminating the intentional pedagogy that was at play within the summer seminar. Hinged upon a belief in raising youth consciousness, the move toward critical research questions was not something that "just happened." Instead, there was a process of peer and adult review of crafted research questions, multiple periods of refinement, and research trajectories outlined long before school groups were given the go-ahead to conduct interviews, distribute surveys, and document their school environments with video cameras, camera phones, and written notes. This process was not put in place to squelch student creativity but to ensure that the questions youth were asking were being approached with the same kind of academic rigor and given the same kind of scrutiny as research undertaken by adult researchers.

Prior to finalizing their research questions, students spent significant time during the first week of the summer seminar offering critiques of the various questions generated by each of the research teams. Conducted in a familiar gallery-walk style, students approached pieces of chart paper posted around the Law School classroom containing draft research questions. Students were given clear directions for providing useful feedback to other teams, including:

- Read the research question as a group
- Underneath the question, write down the topic(s) you feel the question is addressing
- Next, write down different methods you believe the group can use to answer this question
  - o What information do they need?
  - o Who do they need to talk to?
  - o What do they need to find out?

Research teams reviewed the feedback to further revise their questions. And finally, they locked down their questions for the summer. (See Table 4.1 for the summer 2010 research questions.)

TABLE 4.1 Summer Seminar 2010 Research Questions

Team Research Topic	Research Questions
Teaching	What quality of teaching should every child in California be entitled to? Who are the various parties responsible for these entitlements?
Resources	What learning resources do all stakeholders in education believe every student needs in order to receive a high quality education?
Leadership	What is educational leadership? What roles do these leaders play, and who defines accountability?
Social/Physical Environment	How do the social and physical ecologies of schools and communities affect the state of education in California? Have the social and physical ecologies of schools in low-income communities of color changed since the *Williams* case in 2000?
Curriculum	What kind of curriculum does every student in California deserve? What kind of curriculum are we actually getting and why? How are individuals demonstrating acts of courage in the area of curriculum?

It is important to note that these were not static questions—they changed over the course of the school year as students collected data and gained new insights into their topics. For example, the group exploring leadership became very interested in the concept of "organic leadership" based on comments they heard from folks they interviewed over the summer and their reading of Antonio Gramsci's philosophical writings about "organic intellectuals" (1971/1999). As a result, their research question seven months later became, "How can we develop organic leaders? What would it mean if an entire school would be developing organic leaders? Why is it not a priority for schools to develop organic leaders?"

While subsequent chapters of this book will focus on the journey that these questions took the Council on, we want to pause here to emphasize the cyclical process of questioning, researching, reflecting, and re-questioning. It was only through student inquiry—driven by their own lived experiences and the social science literature the group unpacked collectively—that the Council's research questions emerged. It is from these instantiations of student *wonder* that pathways toward action, social justice, and powerful and empirically sound research were birthed.

Conclusion

From reading theory to formulating research questions, this chapter has focused on the iterative processes of asking, developing, and reflecting. The key process here, as in Freire's model of praxis, was the reflecting. The reflection prompts, such as the one that elicited the responses that began this chapter, were not simply lip service to academic work. Instead, these reflections and the discussions they invited introduced the difficult questions and assumptions that were ultimately brought to bear on critical research within the Council.

Consider the structure for doing YPAR that we began constructing in the last chapter. First and foremost, YPAR is built upon the relational trust between community members. From this mutual trust in the process of collaboration and inquiry, YPAR encourages students to see their own experiences reflected (or ignored) in existing forms of research. Their engagement with the research tradition and their insider knowledge about the student experience of schooling prepares them to formulate and refine empirical research questions. Finally, with research questions in hand (as well as the tacit understanding that these questions may change and adapt over time), YPAR pushes students to figure out *how* to answer the complex, pressing questions they have developed. This process, too, is one of mutual exploration, practice, and negotiation. We will discuss the YPAR methodology enacted in the Council in the next chapter.

References

Beers, K. (2002). *When kids can't read: What teachers can do: A guide for teachers 6–12*. Portsmouth, NH: Heinemann.

Crenshaw, K. (2002). The first decade: Critical reflections, or "A foot in the closing door." *UCLA Law Review, 49,* 1343–1372.

Freire, P. (1970). *Pedagogy of the oppressed*. New York: The Seabury Press.

Gramsci, A. (1999). *Selections from the Prison Notebooks*. (Q. Hoare and G. N. Smith, Eds. and Trans). New York: International Publishers. (Original work published 1971)

Matsuda, M. (1991). Voices of America: Accent, antidiscrimination law, and a jurisprudence for the last reconstruction. *Yale Law Journal, 100,* 1329–1407.

Moll, L., Amanti, C., Neff, D., & Gonzalez, N. (1992). Funds of knowledge for teaching: Using a qualitative approach to connect homes and classrooms. *Theory Into Practice, XXXI*(2), 132–141.

Ogbu, J. U. (1995). Cultural problems in minority education: their interpretations and consequences—part two: case studies. *The Urban Review, 27*(4), 271–297.

Philip, T. M., Way, W., Garcia, A., Schuler-Brown, S., & Navarro, O. (2013). When educators attempt to make "community" a part of classroom learning: The dangers of (mis)appropriating students' communities into schools. *Teaching and Teacher Education, 34,* 174–183.

Ruitenberg, C. (2009). Educating political adversaries: Chantal Mouffe and radical democratic citizenship education. *Studies in Philosophy and Education, 28*(3), 269–281.

Yosso, T. (2005). Whose culture has capital? A critical race theory of community cultural wealth. *Race, Ethnicity and Education, 8,* 69–91.

FIGURE 7 A Council student from Wilson High School presents a youth-developed definition of quality teaching

FIGURE 8 Council students from Manual Arts High School demand more powerful curriculum for young people in Los Angeles schools

INTERLUDE

Reflecting on the Council's Pedagogy

In this interlude, Nicole talks with three classroom teachers—Fred David, Eddie Lopez, and Veronica Garcia Garza—who led Council teams at their schools. The conversation reveals the various pedagogical strategies that teachers used to guide their students through the YPAR process and the lasting impact that the Council has had on teachers' personal and professional lives.

Nicole: What was your pedagogical style? What strategies did you use every time you brought these students together to do this research? What were the ways you got students engaged in this work, and how was it similar to or different from what you did in the classroom?

Veronica: Whatever it was we were reading or looking at, the students always had a voice in analyzing a text or sharing their concerns. We brought these texts to them, like Freire or Solorzano—and just like we would do in our classrooms, I think, we helped them to break them down, line-by-line or a chunk here and a chunk there. We then gave students the opportunity to analyze them and to think about what the ideas meant for themselves and their peers. I appreciated that a lot because I think it helped me get better in the classroom. Doing those steps with a small group of kids after school in my classroom, I was like, okay, I can bring Freire into my regular English classroom and we can do it in a very similar way. So the opportunities that our students in the Council got I think we could extend to the rest of our students little by little. As an English teacher, the modeling, the breaking things down, the analyzing, allowing them to deconstruct text—I think those would be my main strategies.

Eddie: One of the great things about our meetings was that we had graduate students there. I worked with Dr. D'Artagnan Scorza—he and I worked very closely as a team for a couple of years. That helped me to flesh out some of the graduate-level readings we were giving our students, to really get in and understand the major concepts and ideas. Even as a graduate of the UCLA graduate program in education, I would struggle, so we would struggle together. It was beautiful to see the students reading Paulo Freire, the Solorzano and Bernal reading, the Yosso, and on and on and on, and having them really see how they applied to their real lives—the relevance and moving from just being academic scholars to developing civic agency. What are the next steps that we see that we want for our community? That's what we would do on a weekly basis. It just varied—sometimes we'd do more of the education theory reading, a lot of the graduate-level reading that you all would kick down to us. But yeah, that's what it looked like on a weekly basis.

Fred: For me, it changed from the summer to the school year. In the summer we had all day, whereas after school our time was limited. So for me it became an issue of time management. We have to present in February, so that means we have this many weeks to get this done, and mapping out what that would look like. So for me deadlines were really important, because if we didn't have them set, then a lot of the work sat on the fence. And sometimes the work sat on the fence up until that last month, and when we got to December we were like, oh, we really need to do these interviews now! So I think especially for the after school meetings it was all about time management, and I had the benefit of having students who had done the program over the summer, so they already had an idea of what to expect.

I think what it came down to was the shorter amount of time and trying to condense work that usually took us five straight weeks into what seemed like a longer stretch of time, but that had less days of time to work with. So one of the most important things was time management. That strategy was really effective. And given the fact that most of the students already had an idea of what they needed to be doing, what the process looked like, it was just a matter of getting it done. My way of enforcing that was the deadlines. I knew that if I didn't get it done, you [Nicole] would come at me with these deadlines, like, Fred, it's been blah blah blah blah blah. [laughing] We need the surveys. We need the surveys. [laughing] So at least from the after school standpoint, it was all about time.

Nicole: I'd like to hear from each of you about what this work has meant to you and how it still influences you today.

Eddie: I think going off of what Veronica and Frederick were speaking about regarding finding those students who were very politically and socially active or the disengaged students who you know have potential in them, I realized that I really was working with the cream of the crop at Roosevelt. It was great for them with what they were benefiting and reaping, all of the experiences and locations that we took them to, like AERA [American Educational Research Association]. I was torn about how I could bring it into the classroom. So the continuing impact that this has had for me and my curriculum is that I have now included YPAR in my classroom for the past three years.

So the 11th grade service learning project—the service learning requirement that is mandated for students in California to graduate—we'd do that in the 11th grade social studies class at Roosevelt. After all of the testing, we had a good solid month left at the end of the school year, so what we started to do was doing YPAR, and I do that 100% now with all of my juniors. I have about 100 students, and I've been doing it for three years now with a 100% completion rate. They're meeting their service learning requirement in addition to taking on topics using the YPAR method. One of the highlights is that at the end they present their work to their fellow peers and the administration. One year, Dr. Solorzano even came out to look at their presentations and give them good critical feedback. And it was fun, because some students, when they would quote, they would quote him! Like, according to *you, you* say that, as they were going into their presentations. It was really cool to see that.

And then they've been pushing it even further. They've been like, we should take this to the faculty at our site; we should be presenting to other students. So that's been in my sphere of influence in my classroom. Then the next level is the Politics and Pedagogy Collective that we have at Roosevelt. Veronica, she presented at one of the workshops that we had about a month ago. So we'll be holding our fourth annual conference next year if all goes well. We had the Council there the first year that we had this conference—they presented during one of the keynote presentations. In terms of attendance, we get between 200 and 400 people, and a lot of it is student-driven—student workshops, community organizations, and professors as well. So that's how I've taken it into my classroom and we've taken it into the larger community of Roosevelt and the East Side of Los Angeles.

Veronica: The Council has had a very long-lasting impact on me. It keeps me grounded in student voice. In everything I do, I'm like, what about the students? What about the students? Making sure they have a voice. And just being grounded in social justice, and always putting those concepts and ideas first and foremost. I take that to my job. As an adjunct faculty member, I get to teach a class for pre-service teachers who are just starting out—it's their first class learning about education and what it means. I use Council videos because the pre-service teachers in my class, most of them come from very privileged backgrounds, and all they know is private school and educational success. So when I show them videos of what it's like for students in LA, and some of the projects that we've done, they're just like, whoa. They don't know what to do, because they've never seen—I didn't know it was like that, you know? They've never seen anything like it.

And maybe they won't go to a school in L.A., but even where they are, to go to some of the neighborhood schools and be confronted with some of the challenges they face, how do you respond to what kids are going through when you've never experienced that? I've been able to bring that in. Also, there's a school here where the students do an action research project, and I've had those students come and present to my students to show them what young people can do. Here's what they can do when you give them a chance to identify an issue to study. They're doing this in the English classroom, the social studies classroom—their school really makes an effort to get students to present these yearlong projects at the end of the year. So I think it really opens up the teachers to think, wow, these young people, look at the potential when you give them the opportunity in the classroom. I just try to take it in that way to the pre-service level so they get a sense of what's possible for them as future teachers.

Fred: The students, as they go through this process and this program, they change. And I think that process of change impacts us as well. To scale it down, it keeps me accountable. It keeps me accountable to the idea that if they were to research me and do an observation of my class, I don't want to be the one that they're talking about. Like, this teacher does this and this sucks. So it keeps me accountable in the sense that it keeps me grounded. But also, how do I build them up? How am I empowering them? What are the things I'm doing in my classroom so that all of my students be like a Bernardo, be like a Brian, or be like an Emily, or an Isaiah? What am I doing to make sure that they all have those opportunities to grow?

It kind of reminds me of what Ernest said at one of our last summer sessions. When you do this work, you're going to either shame or inspire people. That resonated with me for a very long time. It kept me reflective, it kept me grounded, and it kept me thinking, what am I doing? Am I hurting or am I helping? I think this program is instrumental to teachers because it gives you a framework for reflection in terms of the overall goal. It also reminded me that when it comes to the Common Core, I think we're ahead of the curve in terms of helping students develop writing that has a claim, reasoning, and evidence. When all of that started to roll out, I was like, I've been doing this. We've been doing this. I thought that was also very helpful as we do these shifts in pedagogy in order for students to be prepared for the Common Core. It's definitely helped me structure my lessons and structure my units. How can we use research methods that are universally accepted? But at the end of the day, it keeps me grounded and it keeps me accountable.

Veronica: I often think about what kind of teacher might I have been had I not had the opportunity to work with the Council. One of the articles that

I've used is the one that you [Nicole] and Ernest wrote about "teachers as civic agents," you know? And not that I would have just conformed to whatever I had to do, necessarily, but I don't think I would have thought as critically about myself as a teacher and about my responsibility to my students and the community without that opportunity. I think more teachers need a semester in which they're engaging in action research before they go into the classroom so they kind of see what is possible for them.

FIGURE 9 Council students conduct interviews in Sacramento during the 2010 summer seminar

5

MAKING METHODOLOGICAL CHOICES

It's mid-week in July. Students and teachers have been at work for hours already in the UCLA Law School classroom that serves as their home base. Though part of the morning time was spent on check-ins, group discussion, and some logistics, presently the room is looking more like a typical college classroom than it has at any point since the seminar began. In front of the room, two graduate students are reviewing principles of educational research methodology. Today, the discussion focuses on quantitative methods—survey questions, Likert scales, and data tabulation.

After a general overview on the methodologies that are going to be covered, much of the remainder of the day is ceded to John Rogers, who goes into the specifics of crafting and conducting a powerful study using survey data. Sharing easily digestible information from a PowerPoint—and encouraging youth to practice their academic note taking skills—John offers a clear rationale for why survey methodology can be a powerful way to explore the kinds of questions that the Council has decided to investigate. John describes the kinds of questions that surveys can help answer and then begins to brainstorm with the Council about what they want to glean from a survey that will be crafted and given to more than 600 students across Los Angeles high schools in the coming weeks.

John shares some correspondence that a former Council group used to invite students to take their survey. Signed by last year's 28 Council students, the brief recruitment note was included with each survey which the previous year's Council distributed. The note encourages youth participation as part of students' civil rights and encourages current members of the Council to remember why they must take their work so seriously:

> Are you tired of being seen but not heard? Or not taken seriously because you are young? Our youth voices should be valued and recognized! We are interested in how our peers use their voices to speak about their daily struggles.

We, like you, are students struggling to survive in schools throughout Los Angeles. We are participating in a summer program at UCLA. We are promoting and encouraging the importance of youth voice and action,

Through this survey, you have a chance to be heard! We will use the information from these surveys to reach out to schools, community, and policy makers in order to create changes. Fill out the survey and let your voice be heard! Thank you in advance for taking the time to be heard . . . as you should always be!

The students jot down notes and prepare to discuss how these principles of research methodology will influence the work that they will undertake over the summer and school year. The afternoon continues to weave scholarship and social justice together. Students develop questions to ask their peers that are grounded in principles of equity.

This vignette offers a glimpse into how methodological knowledge was discussed and shared in the Council. As we'll discuss below, YPAR is not simply "kids doing what researchers do." Instead, this chapter explores how YPAR methodology expands and extends what counts as research and how we evaluate it. We highlight how young people hold unique and powerful positions as researchers and how their unique life experiences count as methodology.

Though a growing body of scholarship offers case studies of YPAR work in action (see Cammarota & Fine, 2008; Ginwright, Noguera, & Cammarota, 2008), we have seen little that places a theoretical emphasis on YPAR *research*. This chapter explores how changing *who* does research fundamentally changes what research is and *how* and *why* it is done. In concluding this chapter, we want to look at how positionalities within the Council and the role of dialogic reflexivity affect the research process and methodologies employed.

As this chapter continues to tell the story of how the Council took up the YPAR process over the course of a school year, we want to emphasize several key points for researchers and educators to consider. In particular, critical research as envisioned by the Council was not about employing new and different "critical methods." Instead, this chapter highlights the ways that traditional research methods (e.g., surveys, interviews, focus groups, participant observation, etc.) were transformed in critical ways for critical purposes through YPAR. YPAR challenges dominant research traditions in many ways, but still finds value in tweaking time-tested means of data collection toward empowering ends. This chapter highlights how these familiar educational research methods were leveraged in new ways and by new researchers for critical action within the Council. In particular, we explore how the enactment of even the most familiar of research methods, such as surveys and interviews, seriously challenge the assumptions of research communities when taken up by youth.

Crucially, students do not simply become mini-adult researchers through engaging in YPAR. Simply replicating what adults do is epistemologically impossible if we consider the contextual, insider perspectives of students conducting research within their own schools and classrooms. What's more, the students and youth doing YPAR work possess a positionality that has not been fully acknowledged within educational research and social science communities. Bluntly, these are individuals who are often the *object* of research, who through critical research can turn this empirical gaze both inward and on crevices of school life that often escape the adult purview. When youth are trusted to collect and analyze data alongside adult researchers, research communities are transformed into more humanizing and intellectually enriching spaces with newfound power to change educational policies and research assumptions.

A Word about Precision

In Chapter 2, we explored the robust theoretical histories of the youth, participatory, and action elements of YPAR; however, what feels more significantly underdeveloped in the history of YPAR is the role that research actually plays. As the title of this book implies, we want to emphasize here that this is a book about *doing* research. The "R" of YPAR must be able to withstand the same methodological scrutiny as any other methodology. At the same time, the process of researching through collaborative work with youth leads to fundamentally different insights and approaches than would be possible otherwise. We write this chapter recognizing that the work of the Council—the playful give and take of knowledge, the insightful questioning of *when* certain methodologies may be more appropriate for answering research questions than others—offers a glimpse into a new educational research paradigm. The work of the Council and other YPAR groups has the potential to change not only who gets to do research, but also what this research says and to whom. Not since models of teacher inquiry began introducing teacher voice into peer reviewed publication venues have the possibilities of educational research been so significantly expanded.

A New Research Paradigm

As we discussed in the last chapter, the research of the Council students had a circular quality to it—the youth regularly drew their research findings from their own experiences and beliefs as members of the very communities they were researching. When they eventually built their presentations for family and friends in Los Angeles or educational researchers in New Orleans, students developed video documentaries and participatory presentations that invited attendees to see and feel their lives inside and outside of school. They spoke from their own experiences as much as they shared data from interviews and surveys.

The impermanence of youth and the too-frequently changing paradigms of youth culture create a layer of cultural dissonance that is often difficult for adult researchers to penetrate. This constantly moving target of youth identity and youth experiences is something that YPAR research is uniquely positioned to capture and highlight. Though ethnographic research may attempt to beautifully reflect the tribulations of kids in schools (Heath, 1983; Kirkland, 2013), these, too, speak from a positionality that—in terms of how they are viewed within traditional academic paradigms—puts them above and isolated from their participants. In this regard, even the basic approaches of asking questions, documenting sites of research, and engaging in dialogue with adults and peers is a fundamentally different process than traditional research and—as we'll explore in later chapters—yields different research findings. As Irizarry and Brown (2014) explain:

> Young people provide unique and vital insights into the perceptions and actions of students and school personnel and the everyday conditions of schooling. This includes how school policies and practices, institutional structures, and interpersonal interactions can, and often do, impede student success. Capitalizing on these important emic perspectives increases the relevance and applicability of research and interventions to the local school context.
>
> *(p. 66)*

Introducing a noticeably different and necessary perspective to educational research—one that scrutinizes K–12 schooling from the point of view of the students in the classrooms—constitutes the kind of paradigm shift that can redefine what kinds of research questions we explore and fund from within the academy (Kuhn, 1962). Though YPAR presently has a long way to go to more fully gain legitimacy within the educational research establishment, this collaborative methodology is one that has the potential to redefine how research is done, what questions we ask, how we (as educational researchers) interact within research communities, and to whom we report our research.

Not Just "Kids Doing What Researchers Do"

Perhaps one of the biggest assumptions we find that people make about YPAR is that it is a process of having kids mirror the research that adults already do in educational spaces. Considering the amount of time, money, and hard work that academics invest in gaining the credentials to conduct research for universities, think tanks, and policy groups, we can understand the concern some may have of youth taking up the research tools traditionally utilized by the research community but not matching the same level of rigor or validity. And besides, these researchers are too young to *really get* the work that they're doing, right? Even when it remains unspoken, we saw this skepticism emerge again and again at conferences when the Council presented. We saw friends and colleagues cross their arms as they watched youth present, confident that they were about to hear something closer to a juvenile book report than something to merit the attention of an audience of Ph.Ds. We believe that this assumption that kids *can't* do the research we expect of adults precludes serious consideration of what youth *can* do differently when they employ the tools of adults for critical and youth-driven purposes.

While the methodologies look similar to what constitutes traditional research approaches, we argue that there is something fundamentally different that takes place when youth undertake the work of enacting research methodologies. Hand in hand with this concern of expertise is also a consideration of what constitutes a critical, "humanizing" (Paris, 2011) methodology in education research. With a driving goal to build "relationships of dignity and care and glimpsing insider understanding across multiple borders of difference" (Paris, 2011, p. 140), Django Paris has introduced the idea of humanizing research and fostered its development in the educational research community (see Paris & Winn, 2014). These critical researchers argue that scholars must *humanize* the methods they use when working with and within historically marginalized communities and populations, reminding them that "humanizing research does not end when the study does" (Paris, 2011, p. 147). Researchers must consider the overarching purpose behind mining a community for data and the extent to which it serves the communities being studied.

Even prior to Paris's articulation of humanizing research, proponents of "Chicana feminist standpoint" theory (Delgado Bernal, 1998) "questioned objectivity, universal foundations of knowledge, and the western dichotomies of mind versus body, subject versus object, objective truth versus subjective emotion, and male versus female" (p. 560). Delgado Bernal's theory illustrates how qualitative data may reflect, respond to, and respect the voices of research participants. Rather than simply collecting quotes, interviews, and focus groups, humanizing research like YPAR allows nuanced, tacit knowledge and experiences to enter into the historically positivist realm of social science. Ultimately, the work of the Council incorporated the heteroglossic, robust nature of contemporary society even when employing traditional methods of data collection.

Even within a framework of collaborative methodological inquiry, the question still emerges: can we really expect youth to develop and implement a polished and critically transformative research methodology? The answer, for the Council, was yes—with assistance. As we have periodically highlighted throughout the book thus far and will again, we must remember that YPAR does not involve youth working in siloed environments away from all adults.

The revolutionary practice of the Council was made possible through the community that was built combining adult and youth knowledge, experience, and perspectives.

As this chapter's opening anecdote highlighted, expertise within the Council was distributed. Knowledge of methodological approaches to research were disseminated, explored, and challenged within this community of practice. Though graduate students and professors like Ernest and John offered historical perspectives and the expertise gained from experience in the academy, the data collection tools that eventually emerged from the students, such as survey questionnaires, were born through the give-and-take of community collaboration. Such collaboration was not simply about youth consuming the knowledge of adults in the seminar. Instead, there existed a continuous dialogue around methods in the summer seminar and throughout the school year. This dialogue took place not only in person, but online as well. For example, in an exchange on Facebook, members of the Locke High School team discussed theory and methodology. At one point, Laurence challenged his student, Frank, to more deeply investigate his thinking related to organic leadership:

Laurence: Can you explain a little more clearly 1) how she was being hegemonic (how do u think gramsci wud break it down), and 2) how are u being counter-hegemonic??

Frank: In my everyday life I feel Gramsci follows me to class. While in English i just happened to notice that the teacher was being hegemonic by telling us students that since she was the teacher that she was right. By, me being the counter hegemonic person i am, i told her that i felt she was being hegemonic and thats when she cut me off. The reason i feel this way is because if too many students were to be informed, there would be an uprising and she would lose power and in the long run lose control of the class.

Examining this dialogue that emerged around methodology, we can see youth thinking through and *owning* the methodological decisions they make. Though coached and guided by the conversations shaped by researchers and teachers, it is important to see how youth agency acts as the beacon guiding what research is taken up and how data is collected.

YPAR Research in Action

In the previous chapter we described the process of developing specific, answerable research questions within the Council. In order to explore these research questions, the Council proceeded in the way most researchers would when approaching their craft. Through discussion, collaboration, and negotiation, the group determined which methods were needed to empirically answer their research questions. Recognizing the transformative goals of YPAR as a research stance, these methodologies were taken up with consideration of how they positioned research participants and the extent to which they encouraged community insight and support. Further, the processes of data collection and analysis were always considered with an eye toward *action*.

As architects of YPAR, we must consider how the *research* undergirds and helps foment *action*. YPAR methodologies must heal, rejuvenate, and inspire not only the schools and communities in which the work takes place, but the researchers who labor over the work. Though taxing and tiring at times, we believe that if we are going to undertake the research process alongside young people, the work *must* proceed within a critical tradition of love and hope.

Though we have so far focused on the work that happened over the summer in the Council, this investment in time funneled into the academic year. Indeed, many of the methods introduced in the summer were refined through the following fall semester.

Over the past 15 years, the Council has experimented with myriad methodological approaches, mirroring the historical shifts of educational research. Lorrie Shepard (2006) notes:

> the growth and development of new perspectives and methods of inquiry has been remarkable. Researchers in education work at the crossroads of multiple disciplines. Because of this interdisciplinarity, we are more aware than most social scientists of the ways in which narrow, disciplinary perspectives shape scholars' understanding of substantial problems. To the extent that we can become adept at thinking about how we would conceptualize a problem if we approached it as a psychologist, a sociologist, or an anthropologist, we will be more insightful than the psychologist, sociologist, or anthropologist each studying exclusively within their own tradition.
>
> *(p. xi)*

The methodological diversity available within the field of educational research demanded that the Council maintain dexterity to quickly shift methodological approaches based on the contexts of a given research question. Methodological decisions emerged through collective dialogue. Students first identified problems they saw and developed questions to explore these problems further. Next, they needed to figure out how to collect the data that would help them answer these questions. But what *is* data? Where does it come from? Challenging the positivist visions of labcoat-like collection of ideal data, the Council adults helped students understand the messiness of collecting data in the *real* world. While there could be idyllic notions of students carefully filling out surveys or answering focus group questions in perfectly profound sentences, collecting data within the Council (as in many school-based educational studies) required parsing meaning from complicated sets of data.

Too often, the students within the Council faced instability in their schools: constantly shifting teaching and administrative faculties; schedules that bended to the whims of mandated tests; erratic uncertainty about school ending times due to safety "lockdowns." To research within these erratic environments required methodologies that offered analytical resilience. As such, the methodologies employed were chosen to offer some stability in analyzing and collecting data when entering the constantly shifting world of urban schools. Below, we list and briefly describe the methodologies most commonly enacted within the Council of Youth Research.

- **Surveys**—Through collecting survey data from various school sites, students were able to perform quantitative analysis of school-specific and citywide student and teacher beliefs. As Berends (2006) notes, "The aim of survey research is to describe relevant characteristics of individuals, groups, or organizations" (p. 623). Surveys were one of the simplest methodological tools for youth to understand and implement.
- **Interviews**—Along with surveys, interviews were the most familiar form of research to many of the Council students. What adults emphasized with students, however, was the idea of the interview process as a dialectical *exchange*: "Because the interview is an interactional relationship, both informant and interviewer are engaged in an ongoing process of making meaning (Kvale, 1996)" (Brenner, 2006, p. 357).
- **Focus Groups**—Building upon students' familiarity with interviews, focus groups allowed students to move more flexibly into collective dialogue with their participants. These conversations, which often involved students mediating talk between their friends and peers, allowed for unique exchanges that adult researchers are often unable to gain, even within the trust-building endeavors of ethnographic participant observation.
- **Discourse Analysis**—The study of "language-in-use" (Gee, 2011, p. 8) allowed the Council to look at how words used by teachers, school leaders, and politicians were encoded with implicit and explicit meaning. They also pushed toward a Critical Discourse Analysis (Fairclough, 2010), examining the power structures embedded within language use. The study of language and discourse became a powerful way for students to parse the assumptions made in disciplinary policies, district technology statements, and notifications sent home to parents.
- **Autoethnography**—Alexander (1999) described autoethnographic research "as a way of reading between the lines of [our] own lived experience and the

experiences of cultural familiars—to come to a critical understanding of self and other and those places where we intersect and overlap" (p. 310). Students used this tool to analyze their schooling experiences through the lens of critical theory and draw meaningful research findings from the content of their own lives.

Again, these methods are similar to those most frequently undertaken by "adult" researchers in peer-reviewed publications, not ones hand-picked because they are *easier* for students to utilize. Council students participated in workshops that gave them opportunities to intellectually explore, challenge, and critique various methods under consideration. The Council adults deliberately taught students that all methodological approaches have certain shortcomings and that methods should be chosen based on the kinds of questions being asked and sorts of data being sought.

We must again acknowledge that these methods in and of themselves are not inherently critical; however, they take on additional power when they are used to answer critical questions and ultimately lead to critical demands from young people. These tools are standard for social science because they can offer such clear information. The Council relied on these proven methods to support critically grounded research.

While the above methodological approaches were the ones most frequently used, several Council groups began to explore new methods during the 2010–2011 school year. The school group that originated at Manual Arts High School, for example, began to explore more reflective, interior methodologies. They explored the concept of andragogy—the process of adult learning—in order to explore how young people might teach teachers to better meet the needs of their students. This example highlights how the tools of research are not "fixed" either in the Council or for researchers in general. As students follow their lines of critical inquiry, they utilize the analytic tools that are necessary for their journeys.

Moving beyond the Traditional

While the Council's research utilized largely traditional methods, it is important to recognize that these methods fundamentally changed when they were employed by a group of researchers who had been historically disregarded as legitimate researchers within the history of educational research. When youth become researchers through YPAR, the possibilities of what research looks like are challenged and oftentimes shattered. For example, consider the vignette at the start of this chapter and the language Council youth used to encourage their peers to take their survey. This was not simply about recruitment, but about allowing peers' voices to be heard as they "should always be." This was an intentionally transformative process, as students actively advocated for themselves and demonstrated how research could be a legitimate avenue for participation and action.

This work expands the notion of research. Employing traditional methods with non-traditional researchers is non-traditional. Collaborative research practice forces us to re-evaluate our core beliefs as a research and teaching community. What does it mean to interview an individual for research, to conduct a focus group within a local school community? The process of *talking* to other people and of *listening* to responses can look, sound, and feel different depending on the participants. How does research look different when different people are doing it? The focus groups that the Council conducted, for example, might look like nothing more than group conversations taking place at the lunch tables at school or as formal as carefully arranged chairs in a silenced room. For the Council, the *invisibility* of the research process to those outside of it can be a tactical strategy when collecting data that can be damning about the educational practices within urban schools. In this sense, YPAR challenges researchers to consider what happens when multiple perspectives are brought in and the spectrum of *who* does research expands.

Positioning Research as Vulnerable Dialogue

In "The Space Between Listening and Story-ing: Foundations for Projects in Humanization," Valerie Kinloch and Timothy San Pedro (2014) describe the process of writing collaboratively: "we purposefully merged our ideas and moved beyond our own words as knowledge was created in the space between (leading the way to a shared understanding of co-authoring and storying)" (p. 33). Elaborating further on this process, Kinloch and San Pedro describe that they write to intentionally engage their readers and invite them to reveal "vulnerabilities and stories" (p. 34).

Kinloch and San Pedro's focus on vulnerability offers the crucial reminder that YPAR projects work closely with young people during a time of significant biological, social, and cultural development and change in their lives. The process of developing a critical consciousness can be a treacherous one. The process of developing survey items or interview questions with young people about the issues affecting their lives can be painful when they tap into unmet needs. Consider these statements from the survey Council students created in the summer seminar (see complete survey results in Appendix C):

- My teachers care about me and prepare me for the future.
- My teachers are often observed by my administration.
- My teachers communicate well with my parents.

- My teachers value my culture and ideas through their teaching.
- My teachers are excellent.

Students could respond: Strongly Agree, Agree, Disagree, Strongly Disagree. The questions here adhered to the empirical requirements of social science research, but they also had the potential to unearth stinging realizations about the resources and relationships that students deserve but do not receive. While such a data collection instrument could in some contexts cause pain to students, it is transformed due to two key aspects of YPAR methodology. First, students' indigenous community knowledge serves as a guide to the research and speaks back to deficit portrayals of urban youth of color. And second, the process of *doing* research led by youth is one that is about building solidarity and trust with peers. Instead of inspiring anger, frustration, or disengagement, YPAR research, even when revealing unacceptable inequality, offers possibilities and hope for change.

Conclusion: Patient Impatience

Freire's *Pedagogy of the Oppressed* (1970) states that educators must exude "patient impatience." We question how we can be patient or how our students can be patient in the face of oppressive realities of their own schooling. The process of engaging in critical research, for these students, is about honoring the voices of those who are often excluded from research. In the next chapter we will give specific examples of where students go when conducting their research and who they talk to in order to collect data. The *in situ* moment-to-moment process of data collection is dizzying. When distributed among dozens of individuals across a handful of schools, it can feel overwhelming. However, we want to recognize that intentionality around methodology within YPAR can act as the lynchpin for the future steps of this work. If students are able to clearly articulate *why* they are collecting data and can speak to *how* they will do this and continually return to their research questions, they will not lose sight of their overarching purpose during the chaos of fieldwork. Returning to the purposes of a group like the Council, we are reminded by Irizarry and Brown (2014) that:

> Ideally, local researchers participate in every stage of the PAR process: identifying problems; designing the study and instruments; collecting, analyzing, and presenting data; and carrying out action. Through action, PAR researchers implement strategic interventions into the problem(s) under study. Action can take different forms (e.g. teach-ins, workshops, symposia, rallies, and art exhibits) but should be authentic and relevant to the study objectives and findings and to the community's needs, concerns, interests, and ways of knowing and communicating.

(p. 65)

The authenticity and relevance of YPAR work is not found only in the culminating research findings. It is also found in the humanizing methodologies that speak to indigenous, too often oppressed student experiences.

References

Alexander, B. K. (1999). Performing culture in the classroom: An instructional (auto) ethnography. *Text and Performance Quarterly, 19,* 307–331.

Berends, M. (2006). Survey methods in educational research. In J. L. Green, G. Camilli, P. B. Elmore, & American Educational Research Association (Eds.), *Handbook of complementary methods in education research* (pp. 623–639). Mahwah, NJ: Lawrence Erlbaum Associates.

Brenner, M. E. (2006). Interviewing in educational research. In J. L. Green, G. Camilli, P. B. Elmore, & American Educational Research Association (Eds.), *Handbook of complementary methods in education research* (pp. 357–359). Mahwah, NJ: Lawrence Erlbaum Associates.

Cammarota, J., & Fine, M. (Eds.). (2008). *Revolutionizing education: Youth participatory action research in motion.* New York: Routledge.

Delgado Bernal, D. (1998). Using Chicana feminist epistemology in educational research. *Harvard Educational Review, 68,* 555–582.

Fairclough, N. (2010). *Critical discourse analysis: The critical study of language* (2nd ed.). Harlow, England: Longman.

Freire, P. (1970). *Pedagogy of the oppressed.* New York: Herder and Herder.

Gee, J. P. (2011). *An introduction to discourse analysis: Theory and method* (3rd ed.). New York: Routledge.

Ginwright, S., Noguera, P., & Cammarota, J. (Eds.). (2008). *Beyond resistance! Youth activism and community change.* New York: Routledge.

Heath, S. B. (1983). *Ways with words: Language, life, and work in communities and classrooms.* New York: Cambridge University Press.

Irizarry, J., & Brown, T. (2014). Humanizing research in dehumanizing spaces: The challenges and opportunities of conducting participatory action research with youth in schools. In D. Paris & M. T. Winn (Eds.), *Humanizing research: Decolonizing qualitative inquiry with youth and communities* (pp. 63–80). Thousand Oaks, CA: SAGE Publications Inc.

Khun, T. (1962). *The structure of scientific revolutions.* Chicago: University of Chicago Press.

Kinloch, V., & San Pedro, T. (2014). The space between listening and story-ing: Foundations for projects in humanization. In D. Paris & M. T. Winn (Eds.), *Humanizing research: Decolonizing qualitative inquiry with youth and communities* (pp. 21–41). Thousand Oaks, CA: SAGE Publications Inc.

Kirkland, D. (2013). *A search past silence: The literacy of young black men.* New York: Teachers College Press.

Kuhn, T. (1962). *The structure of scientific revolutions.* Chicago: The University of Chicago Press.

Kvale, S. (1996). *InterViews.* Thousand Oaks, CA: Sage.

Paris, D. (2011). *Language across difference: Ethnicity, communication, and youth identities in changing urban schools.* Cambridge, UK: Cambridge University Press.

Paris, D., & Winn, M. T. (Eds.). (2014). *Humanizing research: Decolonizing qualitative inquiry with youth and communities.* Thousand Oaks, CA: SAGE Publications Inc.

Shepard, L. A. (2006). Preface. In J. L. Green, G. Camilli, P. B. Elmore, & American Educational Research Association (Eds.), *Handbook of complementary methods in education research* (pp. xi-xii). Mahwah, NJ: Lawrence Erlbaum Associates.

FIGURE 10 A packed audience listens to the Council presentation at Los Angeles City Hall

FIGURE 11 Nicole addresses Council students before their summer seminar presentation at Los Angeles City Hall

INTERLUDE

Transforming Practice and Identity in the Council

In this conversation, Nicole speaks with Katie Rainge-Briggs, one of the teachers who led a Council team during the 2010–2011 school year. Their talk explores how YPAR challenges traditional ideas of teaching and learning by opening spaces for love and community. Katie shares how the Council inspired her to write an application to start a pilot school with her colleagues. That application led to the creation of Augustus Hawkins High School, which opened in the fall of 2012.

Nicole: When you learned about what YPAR was, whether you had another name for it beforehand or not, did it fit with your existing philosophy of teaching and learning or did it open up something new to you that you hadn't thought about before?

Katie: After this experience, I can't believe that I ever did anything but YPAR. This experience was what I like to believe was an "externship" that extended my Master's program. I mean, I almost feel selfish over how much education I received through this. I've always understood critical race theory. I've always understood why I'm in the business of education, but I don't think I had the tools to properly execute a lesson that put students first and negotiate through difficult texts with all types of learners, with all types of language abilities, until then.

Nicole: It sounds like it was a model of teaching for you as much as it was a model of learning for your students.

Katie: I think that it was a model of education for me but it was a cultural shift for the students. Having the privilege of watching young people in a safe place become aware in high school instead of not experiencing that until college, when all of a sudden they become aware and they don't know what to do with either their privilege or their oppression. It changed who I am as an educator. I think it put me on the path of school reform.

I don't think I would have had enough conviction to write a plan for a pilot school before this experience—I remember saying, "I don't ever want to be a part of pilot school." As a person who believes in unions, I couldn't do it. But this experience in the Council is what made me say, "You know what, I keep talking about what a school should be like, so why don't I just design it based on this research?"

Nicole: What has the journey been like to try to bring YPAR to other spaces after the Council like Hawkins?

Katie: Mass producing YPAR is difficult. But I think that having had that YPAR experience, I got ahead of the game of the Smarter Balanced testing [Common Core–aligned standardized test provider]. I got ahead of the game of Common Core because after the Council explored what powerful youth voice looked like. I was able to use those ideas to guide my professional development for the following year. I focused on the power of youth voice in the classroom. What I realized is that to try to replicate the YPAR experience, a couple of things have to happen. First, there has to be a phase where kids get to be off their oppressive campus sites. Now, here, we don't like to call our school oppressive, but in high school when you're around the same group over and over again, you get typecast. Removing them from that situation allows them to redefine themselves. It also allows the concentration time, the focus time. It allows them to be around intellectuals for chunks of time. I think that gave the Council experience depth. It became an apprenticeship program. Now, when we do it here, I realize, even though I have it in small groups, they lack the apprenticeship. That is one of the biggest problems of replicating a YPAR model in school like the one we had in the Council.

In terms of adult research, now I look at you like you're crazy if you do research without the researcher's experience and voice in it.

Nicole: I feel like all the teachers in the Council had their own styles. They took YPAR to a place that was important for them. Your group, you focused a lot on caring during that 2010–2011 school year. You started going beyond the traditional PowerPoint research presentation and playing with song and with spoken word. When did you get to a point where you started feeling like you wanted to play with alternative research methods?

Katie: I was thinking a lot about how we as students when we become hip to something, when we become aware of something, we kind of look at our families like, "You don't know. Now, I know." I think that it is so important that if we honor different types of learners, we have to honor different types of teachers in our lives. I think that, looking back, I must have gone on a personal journey. I realized that my first lessons in democratic learning and educational advocacy were from my mom. And then, when the summer seminar started that year, I had just had a baby. Watching his development and coming home every day to a boy of color, I think why I had this song in my head that I shared with the students that year— "Everybody Is a Star" by Sly and the Family Stone.

I think that the Council just gave me an opportunity to integrate what's always been around me into the research process. Music is such a big part of my culture. Being a New Yorker, being African American, being Puerto Rican, that is the way we were able to hold onto a story when the story wasn't told by mass media—we told it through hip hop, through merengue, through gospel. All that different stuff. I had that moment of praxis, right where your pedagogy meets your theory and then all of a sudden, ta-da! But I think it was all about timing, timing, timing.

Nicole: What was it like in those meetings during the school year when you're telling these stories to your students and trying to help them to understand the ethic of caring and love for each other and love for their ancestors? What were the ups and downs? What do you remember about getting that group to the place that they got to by the time we got to AERA?

Katie: I remember wishing we were in boarding school because every time they left me, they took on an old hat that just didn't fit them anymore but that they didn't know how to let go of. I remember thinking, if only their teachers understood to hold the bar higher. If only their classmates understood that they have these leaders among them. I remember really being afraid they were going to miss out on an opportunity because I don't think anyone ever is ready for the information coming at them. But I think that that was the year. I really did have students with amazing abilities. I think that if I had caught them in elementary school, they would all been considered gifted and talented.

But the personal journeys they took affected them so much. It was so difficult to battle the outside world just to get their concentration. That group underestimated themselves. That's also why I realized that I had to do a better job of sharing the power and process of YPAR with colleagues and that I needed the space committed to that. That's how I realized that I had to create that space, which is how my small school at Hawkins, the Responsible Indigenous Social Entrepreneurship (RISE) learning academy, was born. Because the students would get eaten up again by the school system when the summer ended.

Nicole: I remember you talking that year about what it meant to be a teacher after becoming a mother. We often don't talk about love in educational spaces, but there was always a lot of talk about love in your group. I wonder how the students responded to this idea of love in the group. Did they push it away at first? What was that journey like, and how did it influence you?

Katie: This is exactly why I now use restorative justice as my new pedagogy—it's my method of cognitive coaching through the concept of love. At first, when I tried to discuss that, colleagues would say, "That's that touchy feely curriculum." I was having a lot of trouble trying to give people steps, to articulate what it meant to replicate this concept of love in the classroom. I think restorative justice gives me the words to do that. But I wouldn't have discovered restorative justice unless I had been on that path from the Council. It did put me on that path. Again, ethnography does that. When you give kids the space to talk about what makes them who they are, you learn so much that changes how you act and how a school looks and feels.

Nicole: Can we say that the Council created the Hawkins? [laughing]

Katie: [laughing] You laugh, but during our first year when we were being interviewed by the accreditation panel, I told myself, I'm not going to cry at a really serious moment like this, but the question came up, "How do you all do it? I just don't see how you all do it." All of a sudden, something came over me and I said, "We didn't do it. There's a collective of people who helped create this and they're not at the table right now. Some of them are not even in the city. Some of them not even in the state, but there's a collective." And that's why sometimes when I feel like at Augustus Hawkins we forget who we are or where we've come from, I remind them that we are dedicated to community action.

We were dedicated to community action before we even had a building. That was because all of us had this experience that the Council was able to give us—that light. We saw what could be and had to figure out how we could try to replicate this for every child.

FIGURE 12 Council teacher, Katie Rainge-Briggs, praises students before their spring presentation at the UCLA Labor Center

6

BECOMING RESEARCHERS THROUGH DATA COLLECTION AND ANALYSIS

Watching a group of 16-year-olds who just yesterday were confidently analyzing a complex scholarly article suddenly clam up and hesitate to approach a ninth grader to ask for an interview makes me laugh (inwardly, of course). This happens every year—the self-assurance that students feel as they are learning about research theories and methods in the classroom quickly dissipates into nervousness during their first day actually conducting research in the field. I can laugh because I know that this is part of the learning curve and that these same students will fearlessly approach random adults on the street for interviews in just a few more days.

I am standing in the Manual Arts High School courtyard during lunchtime. Students enjoying the break between their summer classes stream across the yard, perching on metal tables or sitting on the ground in tight circles to eat and gossip. Within the crowd I can spot the CYR students easily from the blue name badges around their necks. They are the ones poking their fellow team members, trying to work up the courage to approach students and ask their prepared interview questions as one of their teacher leaders prods them to "stop being silly and just ask anyone."

I move closer to the team researching how students define quality teaching. I watch as Patricia, the shortest and spunkiest member of the group, finally sidles up to a student and says, "We're part of the UCLA Council of Youth Research and we're students from L.A. who want to give students a voice in their own education. Could we ask you a few questions about your teachers for our research?" The student shoots a sidelong glance at the video camera that Gustavo has hoisted up onto his shoulder, but shrugs and agrees. The team members, a bit flustered now that they realize that this is actually happening, flip open their notebooks and settle into their roles. Carolina stands behind Gustavo so that she can mark times during the interview that she wants to pick out for transcription and Evelyn prepares to ask the first question: "What do you think are the qualities that a 'good' teacher has to have?"

After a brief pause, the student haltingly begins to share. I step back and take the scene in—a group of young people furiously taking notes as one of their peers talks about an issue they all care deeply about. The Council students nod and ask follow-up questions—they are really listening. I could swear that the team members start to stand up straighter as the interview continues and they begin to realize that it's really happening—they are becoming researchers.

Nicole wrote this vignette while observing Council students as they collected data "out in the field" for the first time with their team members and adult mentors during the 2010 summer seminar. While subsequent field days were tailored to each team's particular research interests, with adults driving carloads of students to various locations around the city, this first field day involved the entire Council. The adult mentors carefully crafted the agenda for this day, mindful that many students were nervous about approaching young people and adults with video cameras to ask them sensitive questions about their educational experiences. They wanted students to visit locations that would inform their research projects, but they also wanted to make sure that students had a positive experience that expanded their perspectives about themselves and their city. The goal was for students to begin to see themselves as part of a team of researchers and to see their schools and their city as a site to be critically analyzed.

The agenda that was decided upon for the inaugural field day first brought the Council to Manual Arts High School, a school in South Los Angeles that some of the Council's students attended. The student teams fanned out across the school—the Leadership group interviewed the principal, while the Environment group observed the campus aesthetics, and the Teaching group sought out students to interview about their favorite and least favorite classes. Starting at Manual Arts was a strategic choice aimed at easing students into their roles as researchers in a setting that felt more familiar to them, considering that the Council students, if they did not attend Manual Arts themselves, attended schools that looked and felt very similar in terms of the composition of the student body and the level and quality of resources.

Since the research theme for the summer involved analyzing inequitable educational resources across and between different schools in California, adults decided that the next stop should be Beverly Hills High School, a school environment that represented the most drastic possible counterpoint to the one students had experienced at Manual Arts and yet was only 12 short miles away. While students engaged in research activities at Beverly Hills that mirrored those they had engaged in at Manual Arts, the sharp change in context—virtually all of the students had never visited this part of the city before—made this an entirely new experience for them as researchers and as adolescents processing their social locations in an unequal society.

Adults interested in designing YPAR experiences have consistently approached us to ask a wide array of logistical questions about how to go about taking young people out of the formal learning spaces of schools and universities and into the larger community. Indeed, the fact that it often seems so daunting to arrange the necessary permissions and itineraries for out-of-classroom learning speaks to the difficulty of disrupting traditional approaches to teaching and learning. This chapter will provide some nuts-and-bolts guidance about what it takes to organize and implement opportunities for student research "field days" in both school and community spaces. First, however, we will offer insights into the connections between the Common Core State Standards in Literacy and the forms of data collection and analysis that take place in the context of YPAR projects in order to highlight the academic nature of this work and its value in preparing students with college, career, and civic readiness skills. It is this value that makes the work of organizing field days so worthwhile.

While the mechanics of data collection and analysis are important to explore, this chapter also examines the complex ways in which the process of engaging in research influences students' identities. While the previous chapter documented the various methodologies that students were exposed to in the classroom space to help them *conduct* research, this chapter illuminates the journey into the field when students actually *become* researchers. This process of becoming researchers was neither easy nor painless for the Council students, particularly as it pushed them to grapple with how they were viewed by others and the ways in which they themselves were experiencing educational inequities firsthand.

What are the implications of young people declaring themselves producers of knowledge—particularly young people of color living in marginalized communities? How do young people understand and manage the tension they face collecting data in their own communities and balancing their identities as both insiders and outsiders? What about the tension of trying to become insiders in spaces which try to keep them outside? This chapter explores the ways that YPAR is not simply a practice of young people mimicking adult researchers in the field, but instead a radical re-envisioning of what research is, who does it, and why it matters.

Honing Academic and Civic Skills through Data Collection

What Council students do can be better understood as a revolutionary learning experience when examined within the current context of literacy education.

The introduction to the Common Core State Standards for English Language Arts indicates that reading, writing, listening, and speaking skills are "essential to both private deliberation and responsible citizenship in a democratic republic" (National Governors Association, 2010, p. 3). The introduction to the standards produced by the International Reading Association and the National Council of Teachers of English also stresses that failure to prepare students with advanced literacy skills undermines "our democratic ideal" (National Governors Association, 2010, p. 6).

Despite these positive intentions, many of the ways that literacy is currently operationalized in schools hinder rather than support a focus on civic engagement. In an exhaustive review of eleven recent adolescent literacy reports, Faggella-Luby, Ware, & Capozzoli (2009) found that policymakers consistently operate from a narrow definition of adolescent literacy focused on academic reading skills that prepare students for postsecondary school and work—one that creates little space for students to "think critically about the world they inhabit and develop their own alternative literacies" (p. 470).

One consequence of this narrow definition of literacy has been the construction of the "struggling reader" and the marginalization of the literacy practices of students from non-dominant communities (Alvermann, 2006). The use of "deficit" and "difference" pedagogies in recent decades demonstrates that the teaching of academic literacies is often equated with the eradication of or willful blindness to the language and cultural forms of expression that students of color bring to the classroom (Paris & Ball, 2009). Further, the results of 2013 National Assessment of Educational Progress (NAEP) showed that these "narrowing" literacy practices are not diminishing socioeconomic achievement gaps; while 47% of White and Asian-American 12th graders scored proficient or higher in reading, only 23% of Hispanic and 16% of Black 12th graders did the same (National Center for Education Statistics [NCES], 2014).

Of course, civic education as it is traditionally conceptualized shares similar problems. Civic standards are often vague, overly reliant on factual knowledge, and impossible to achieve in the given time frames (Gagnon, 2003). In addition, civic education curricula often utilize patriotic, triumphalist rhetoric that ignores the experiences of communities of color and "do not connect to their own identities as citizens" (Torney-Purta & Vermeer, 2004, p. 14). Such conceptualizations of citizenship rarely acknowledge legacies of systemic discrimination in housing, healthcare, and the criminal justice system that influence how youth of color see their country (Watts & Flanagan, 2007).

By applying reading, writing, speaking, and listening skills to addressing issues of public concern, YPAR offers a unique blend of academic and civic education that broadens narrow academic conceptions of literacy, imbuing it instead with critical purposes of individual and community empowerment. This melding of the academic and civic purposes of literacy comes at a time when the Common Core State Standards in Literacy are sweeping across the country, creating an opportunity for YPAR to become more integrated into schools as a means of helping students develop analytic skills.

It is important to note that the Common Core standards do not explicitly recognize the civic aspects of literacy. While the terms "college" and "career" appear dozens of times in the standards, the 60+ page document mentions democracy exactly twice—in the previously mentioned introduction and in an 11th and 12th grade speaking/listening standard that calls for the promotion of "civil, democratic discussions" (p. 50).

In both cases, the mechanisms through which the skills of reasoning or discussions are meant to connect to democracy (let alone what kind of democracy we are preparing young people for) are left completely unexplored. The standards call for the skills and suggest that they are important for democracy, but do not help teachers or students actually make the connection in any meaningful way. No standards call for students to engage in literacy practices in or with their communities, or to create public literacy products like letters to legislators or public service announcements.

Nevertheless, the general literacy skills that these standards call for can be developed through the activities of data collection and analysis (see Tables 6.1, 6.2, and 6.3).

TABLE 6.1 YPAR and Academic Reading Skills

Standards-Based Academic Skills	YPAR Activities that Meet/Exceed Standards
Reading • Close reading and citation of evidence to support claims • Summarizing themes and key supporting details • Determine technical, connotative, and figurative meanings of words • Analyze text structure and how point of view shapes texts • Evaluate content presented in diverse format and media • Evaluate validity of reasoning and sufficiency of evidence in texts	• Reading and analyzing a variety of documents related to research topics, including: court filings and decisions, scholarly and news articles, infographics, census and state education data, and press releases • Understanding technical vocabulary used in different types of informational texts • Analyzing the various ways that data can be presented based on the point of view of the person or organization presenting it • Evaluating the data used to make particular claims about schools and communities and comparing it among a range of sources

TABLE 6.2 YPAR and Academic Writing Skills

Standards-Based Academic Skills	YPAR Activities that Meet/Exceed Standards
Writing • Write arguments to support claims using valid reasoning and evidence • Write informative texts to examine and convey complex ideas clearly • Produce writing that is appropriate to task, purpose, and audience • Engage in planning, revising, editing, and rewriting • Use technology, including the Internet, to produce and publish writing • Conduct research projects based on focused questions and gather relevant information from print and digital sources	• Writing survey items • Writing interview and focus group questions • Writing observational field notes • Creating PowerPoint presentations and storyboards for documentary films • Analyzing data drawn from a variety of sources and choosing most compelling examples to make arguments • Using different writing styles to effectively communicate with different audiences during presentations • Working with group members to collaboratively write and edit presentations • Publish presentations on blogs, websites, and social media

TABLE 6.3 YPAR and Academic Speaking & Listening Skills

Standards-Based Academic Skills	YPAR Activities that Meet/Exceed Standards
Speaking/Listening	
• Participate effectively in a range of conversations, communicating ideas persuasively • Integrate information presented in diverse media and formats • Make strategic use of visual displays of information • Adapt speech to a variety of communicative tasks and contexts	• Conducting interviews and focus groups • Distributing surveys • Explaining research topic to various stakeholders • Code-switching in speech while talking to various audiences • Working on public speaking skills such as projecting voice, speaking slowly, and speaking with emphasis • Delivering powerful presentations that impact audience members and express research findings persuasively

Consider the skills that students need to find data sources, collect and analyze data, and synthesize findings into a polished presentation. Compare those skills to the skills that students are expected to master during high school according to standards. While we use language from the Common Core standards here, these skills are adaptable to many state and organizational standards.

Students can (and do) gain each of these skills through engaging in YPAR data collection and analysis, and they do so in the context of research about community issues that possess great meaning for them rather than a social vacuum.

Field Day Logistics

To Do List: July 13, 2010—7:30 a.m.–8:30 a.m.

1. *Organize and number the equipment bags for each team—2 voice recorders, 1 digital camera, 1 video camera, 5 tapes, 5 field notebooks, 5 pens, and a handful of batteries.*
2. *Alphabetize permission slips for students to travel in educators' vehicles.*
3. *Review and make copies of the driving list, containing the names and cell phone numbers of every person in every car, making sure that student team members are traveling together with their adult mentors to the same locations.*
4. *Head to the meeting location and do a head count of all students and adults.*
5. *Make sure a representative from each team collects the equipment bags.*
6. *Distribute the minute-by-minute agenda and directions to all field locations.*
7. *Distribute name badges and make sure all students are wearing them around their necks.*
8. *Put bag lunches prepared by UCLA Catering Services in the trunk of my car.*
9. *Supervise as adults pull up in their cars and students pile in.*
10. *Do another head count.*
11. *Drive to Manual Arts High School with students.*

12. *Check in at the front office and send teams to their first appointments (which were made in advance with the principal and various teachers/students).*
13. *Call ahead to appointments scheduled at the next field location to confirm.*
14. *Check in with teams and deal with malfunctioning equipment, missing pens/notebooks, and late appointments.*
15. *Take a deep breath.*

Escorting 30 high school students to locations across the city of Los Angeles is no small logistical feat. Making field days happen is a good reminder that doing YPAR is not always an intellectual activity; sometimes, it is about hardcore organizational skills and getting young people from one place to another safely while meeting their basic needs for food, transportation, and fun. Of course, learning is happening during the in-between moments of waiting at traffic lights and eating lunch, just as it is during the interviews that are the highlights of field days. Mark Bautista, who worked with the Council as a graduate student, termed this learning, "carpool pedagogy," and as much planning went into these outings as the research topics themselves (see *Interlude: Brokering Relationships in the Council* to hear more from Mark).

We'd like to highlight some of the major considerations that need to be taken into account when planning excursions into the field for YPAR data collection.

Adult Planning

Turning the traditional research paradigm on its head and situating young people as the leaders of the research process can easily lead to the idea that young people need to independently control every aspect of data collection, from choosing the individuals to be interviewed to setting up the appointments and developing the interview questions. From this perspective, adult assistance could be construed as an example of robbing students of their agency as researchers.

The Council does not adopt this perspective; on the contrary, as we discussed in Chapter 3, the adults in the group take very seriously their responsibility to use their skills and social networks to facilitate the research process and set students up for success. Considering that the adults in the Council had many connections to educators, community activists, and politicians across the city, they found it inconceivable that they would not utilize these connections to enrich students' research.

Indeed, adults strategically organized data collection opportunities for students in ways that helped them to build confidence and skills, often scheduling the first few interviews with individuals whom they knew interacted well with young people and would be sympathetic to students' concerns. They created scaffolds for the data collection experience during the 2010 Summer Seminar, with students' first experience of filming an interview, asking questions, and taking notes occurring during a teacher panel on the UCLA campus. Adults planned this event in order to help students experience the process of setting up their cameras, assigning roles to group members, and handling unexpected interview responses in the safe environment of their normal meeting room and with friends of the Council.

During their small group meetings, the adult mentors helped students craft interview questions geared toward the specific stakeholders they were set to meet—separate protocols for students, teachers, administrators, community members, and school district officials. They encouraged students to practice the speeches they would give when inviting students to take their survey, and coached them through how to encourage interview subjects to elaborate if they gave short, unsatisfying responses. They brainstormed with students about the types of footage they wanted to make sure they captured and the functions this footage would serve in helping to tell their stories in their documentary films.

Again, the purpose of the adult planning was to demonstrate to students the amount of preparation needed to conduct quality research and to help them anticipate the variety of unexpected obstacles that they might encounter in the messy real world in order to bolster their confidence and keep them engaged in the research process.

Resources

Every YPAR program is unique in terms of the number of students it serves and the community context in which it is situated. The resources needed to successfully collect data are dependent upon these two factors; for instance, the resources that the Council needed as a group of 30 students and 10 adults living in a community that can only be easily traversed by car are much different from those required by a smaller group operating in a location that boasts more convenient public transportation.

In addition to the resources needed to collect and analyze data (audio recording devices, cameras, computers, editing and presentation software), the Council needed to think about resources related to getting around Los Angeles with young people—cars with licensed drivers, signed parent permission slips allowing adults to transport minors, food and drinks to sustain students during daylong trips, and meeting space at UCLA.

The work of the Council was supported by grants awarded to UCLA professors, who used them to provide stipends to the adult mentors, secure meeting space, and purchase the necessary equipment; nevertheless, adults in the program consistently spent money out of their own pockets to supplement these grants and make sure that students' needs were met. Each program must consider its own needs and consider the resources to which it has access.

Flexibility

One of the most important lessons that we have learned from coordinating the work of the Council is the need to be comfortable adapting to changing circumstances and the willingness to take advantage of opportunities that may arise on an impromptu basis.

One such impromptu opportunity that arose during the 2010 summer seminar was a research trip to Sacramento to speak with state officials about the impact of the *Williams* decision. While a visit to the state capital was not planned when the summer seminar began, it became a reality when Ernest and John reached out to legislative staff and realized that many individuals were available and willing to speak with students during the fourth week of the seminar.

Speaking to state legislators about the impact of a state supreme court decision was clearly relevant to students' research and offered a unique opportunity for students to learn more about the levels of government and the voting records of the representatives from their communities. And so we jumped on it. In the course of one week, a coach bus was reserved, hotel reservations were made, and parent permission was secured to bring the entire group on the six-hour overnight trip. (See Table 6.4 for the meetings students attended in Sacramento.)

TABLE 6.4 Sacramento Appointment Calendar

Time	Interviewee	Location	Attending
9 a.m.	Under-Secretary of Education Kathryn Radtkey-Gaither	1121 L Street Suite 600	LT's group Antonio's group
10 a.m.	Chief of Staff for Karen Bass— Nolice Edwards	Capitol Building Room 319	Katie's group Fred's group
10 a.m.	Director of Legislative and Community Affairs, Public Advocate—Liz Guillen	Capitol Building, 6th Floor Cafeteria	Nik's group LT's group Antonio's group
11 a.m.	Education Consultant for Gloria Romero—Roslyn Escobar	Capitol Building Room 2090	Antonio's group Nik's group
11 a.m.	New American Media—Rupa Dev	Will meet us	Dimitri Emily Sofia Erick Evelyn With Ernest
12 p.m.	LUNCH	TBD	
1:30 p.m.	Superintendent Jack O'Connell and State Director of P-16 Division Jose Ortega	1430 N Street Suite 1101	ALL
2 p.m.	Legislative Director for Curren Price—Reggie Fair	Capitol Building Room 2052	Judith Jessica Franklin Frank Carolina With Antonio
2:30 p.m.	Sacramento Mayor Kevin Johnson and Education Initiatives Director Andrea Corso	New City Hall 915 I Street 5th Floor	ALL

The summer seminar was a unique experience due to its length and level of rigor, both of which were made possible by the fact that adults and students were being compensated for their time and could invest five weeks of full-time work into making it successful. Once the school year began, however, this level of investment was simply not possible. Teachers and professors returned to their full-time teaching responsibilities, graduate students returned to classes and work on their dissertations, and students balanced engagement in the Council with their commitments to schoolwork and to other extracurricular activities.

As a result, data collection during the school year as the Council research continued needed to look very different. Students could only meet in their teams one day per week after school with their adult mentor, and they did not have the ability to travel around the city for interviews. The solution that most groups developed to this challenge was to turn inward and spend their time researching the way that their summer research topic played out at their school sites. They interviewed those closest to them—administrators, teachers, and students—and worked with their schools to have entire student bodies take their surveys. Again, flexibility was key in keeping the YPAR process going.

"The Grind"

In all, students participated in eight field days during the 2010 Summer Seminar. They conducted dozens of interviews, snapped hundreds of pictures, filmed hours and hours of video footage, and collected over 600 responses to their survey. (See Appendix C for student survey results.) As they returned from their data collection trip in Sacramento, they felt accomplished. They chattered excitedly during the bus ride home about their success and basked in the praise they had received from adults.

As the bus rolled back into Los Angeles, Laurence interrupted the self-congratulatory mood to make some important announcements that quickly quieted the bus. "You all realize that we only have five days left to turn all of this into a presentation, right? What are you going to do about what you've heard? We call this time 'the grind.'" The students glanced at each other confusedly, wondering what the term meant and why all of the adults on the bus were chuckling and shaking their heads, anticipating the exhaustion to come.

"The grind" is Council shorthand for the data analysis process—the often-tedious, decidedly un-glamorous stretch of time between the fun of data collection and the glory of the final presentation, when the wealth of data needs to be harnessed into a coherent and unified story that will faithfully represent what was found and move the audience to action. It is referred to as "the grind" because that is what it is—days that stretch into nights of reviewing tapes to find that one powerful quote, of figuring out the common themes that underlie what multiple interviewees said, and of mastering the ins and outs of PowerPoint and Final Cut Pro so that these tools will help tell the story that needs to be told.

The five days of data analysis were the days when students and teachers stayed holed up in Law School classrooms until 10 or 11 p.m. Students' bus tokens became useless because the adults wouldn't let them travel home alone at such late hours—carpools were rearranged by neighborhoods as each student was dropped off one-by-one. Drivers wouldn't pull away until parents opened their doors to welcome their children home, bemused that their sons and daughters were willingly putting in 13- and 14-hour days for their research.

Over these five days, the relational bonds that the students and adults formed during the team-building exercises and work in the field are tested as the stress of trying to formulate findings and communicate them to an audience leads to lack of sleep and, in turn, short tempers. The adult mentors strive to organize tasks to avoid the problems that can stem from having too many cooks in the kitchen; they split their groups into PowerPoint and documentary film teams, drawing upon students' natural strengths when making their assignments.

During the "grind" of the 2010 Summer Seminar, students whittled down all of the information they had gained into 10-minute PowerPoint presentations and 5-minute documentaries, drawing from multiple sources to communicate their findings in their final PowerPoints. The ability to selectively choose specific pieces of information in order to persuasively present claims and evidence requires a set of skills needed to succeed in both the academic and civic spheres. (See Table 6.5 for data points used in each student presentation.)

The grind also continued into the school year as the school-based research teams built upon their summer research in preparation for their spring presentation at the American Educational Research Association Annual Meeting. Data collection and analysis presents special challenges during the school year because, as we mentioned earlier, unlike during the summer when students can spend hours on end perfecting PowerPoints and documentary films, the school year puts many additional pressures on students as they balance their classwork, homework, and other extracurricular activities.

Teams compensated for the tighter time frame for completing their research during the school year by restricting data collection to their immediate school sites and reworking existing survey and interview protocols instead of starting from scratch. One aspect of the research process that did not change, however, was the focus on student construction of knowledge. Team leader Laurence explained how, even though it took more time, he insisted that his students do the heavy lifting needed to define and explore their research topic on their own:

> I always take it from where they're coming from. We definitely try to build with them instead of telling them, "Here it is." It started by asking those questions: what does it mean to be a leader? In that group we had a lot of leaders in different ways—we had people who were active in the

TABLE 6.5 Student Presentation Data Points

Group Topic	Data Points
Curriculum	• *Williams* complaint • Education data from UCLA IDEA (number of advanced science and math classes) • Quotes from 2 student interviews • Pictures of classrooms • Census data • Results from 5 survey items
Physical/Social Environment	• Education data from UCLA IDEA (neighborhood racial change, average household income by neighborhood) • Pictures of resources • 2 quotes from teachers • 2 quotes from students • 1 quote from community activist • Results from 4 survey items • 2 book quotes
Leadership	• Pictures from interviews • 1 quote from parent interview • School board schedule • Results from 7 survey items • 3 quotes from teachers • 1 quote from community activist • 1 quote from local superintendent • 3 quotes from books/articles • State education data about Algebra 1 and English test scores
Resources	• *Williams* settlement • Pictures of resources • 2 book quotes • Results from 2 survey items • 2 quotes from principals • 5 quotes from students • 2 quotes from counselors • 2 quotes from teachers • 3 quotes from activists • State education data of school API and AYP • Education data from IDEA (new teachers in LAUSD schools and college opportunity ratio)
Teaching	• CA education code about definition of highly qualified teachers • Education data from IDEA about percentages of highly qualified teachers at LA schools and College Opportunity Ratio • 4 quotes from students • 4 quotes from teachers • Results from 4 survey items

community, we had people who were leaders on their respective sports teams and on their campuses, so we went from there. We asked the questions: who is a leader? Is a leader someone who is born? How can someone become a leader? Just like our research, we wanted them to organically develop their understanding versus telling them, "This is what it is." That took a lot—it really took a lot. We were proud because we said, here's Gramsci. What do you guys take from it? How does this apply?

Nevertheless, Laurence admitted that, as deadlines loomed and presentations approached, organic processes gave way to delegation of tasks and more teacher input; as he put it, "A little bit later, unfortunately, you start running out of time with that development, so we have to hustle. We would strategically break it up and say, okay, this group, you tackle theory; this group is going to focus more on methods." The teams found that flexibility was a key competency to making YPAR work during the times when entire days could not be devoted to the grind, which ended up providing students with additional skills in collaboration and time management.

Navigating the Researcher Identity

"The first field day made me feel confident about myself to obtain good data regarding my research topic. I did not feel shy or uncomfortable approaching people, introducing myself, introducing the Council, and asking them if they would like to be interviewed."

Evelyn, 12th grader

"I learned so much on how urban and suburban areas differ. For example, teens in urban areas say that they do not get enough resources, while suburban teens say that they get all the resources they need. They said they get so many resources that they often get confused because some of those resources are not even needed. That really made me think—we have few resources in urban schools, while suburban schools have so much that even kids start to ask: why so much? That question was so powerful to me. It also made me think there was no balance in resources—because rich schools ask for less while we ask for more, but yet we still do not get any resources. So that makes me feel sad that still very few people make the effort to make a change in schools for OUR education."

Franklin, 11th grader

"From the first field day it was very interesting how the people that live in different communities act or behave in front of people that don't live there. For most of the time I felt that in Manual Arts High School, you could actually have the confidence to speak with people. On the other hand, when we went to Beverly Hills High School, the people in there would look at us as if we were people from another planet and that we shouldn't be around them because we were not from that specific area. This made me think that it is our turn to go and fight for our rights to a better education and for more respect for who we are and where we come from. Now it is my turn to stand up and fight for my people's rights and for everyone else."

Gustavo, 11th grader

"People around the school kept looking at us as if we didn't belong."

Carolina, 11th grader

"The first day I thought was really fun and kind of nerve wracking. When we went to Beverly Hills High School I sort of felt out of place, like I didn't really fit in that area—not because the school was predominantly white but because it's not really what I'm used to doing or where I'm used to being. You can say that these communities are really different in the way they look and the level of luxury. When we went there we saw many tourists. How often do you see a tourist in Watts or South Central?"

Dimitri, 12th grader

Council students wrote these reflections the morning after their first field day, still buzzing with excitement from their first taste of data collection. Their writing reveals that the experience entailed more than simply asking interview questions or video-recording observations; indeed, it spurred students to simultaneously look inward and outward to understand their own identities, the city in which they lived, and the new relationship between the two that being a researcher was forging. When young people of color conduct research in a participatory fashion for the purpose of creating transformative social action in their schools and communities, it is not simply an academic exercise. YPAR represents something more—a process that turns the traditional adult/youth power relationship on its head and offers adolescents an opportunity to engage in authentic critical personal and social analysis.

The first theme that emerges from these reflections is a clear sense that the researcher identity *matters* to students in a way that goes far beyond wearing name badges. Evelyn's comment about the confidence she felt in her ability to gather data for "her" research speaks to the sense of ownership that students had over their self-selected research topics, as well as the way that being a researcher made her feel qualified and poised to approach adults and young people and engage them in conversations around what could easily be seen as controversial social issues. Belonging to a collective of youth researchers lent students the self-assuredness needed to become questioners and knowledge-seekers rather than objects of the educational efforts of adults.

In turn, the adults that students encountered on field days often regarded them with amazement and respect, commenting on the incisiveness of their questions and their professional manner when pursuing information. Interview subjects would often approach us and other adult mentors in the group, impressed at the academic rigor of the students' work and their interest in social issues, eager to learn more about the program.

This was especially true when students had the opportunity to meet with the senior staffers of state senators and assembly members in Sacramento. Since the motivating force behind the summer research agenda was the 10th anniversary of the *Williams v. California* state supreme court filing, state politics had an important role to play in the students' research. Many of the questions that students had about their research topics, from unequal educational resources to qualified teacher shortages and inadequate school facilities, were related to state funding formulas and decisions made by legislators far from their communities and schools. The adults decided that students should be able to ask their questions to the legislators themselves and receive some answers. Students researched the voting records and position statements of the legislators representing their districts and arranged meetings with their education aides or chiefs of staff.

These staffers continued the trend of adults bestowing accolades upon the young researchers. While the students took pride in the praise bestowed upon them, the adult mentors harbored more conflicted feelings about it—they obviously wanted their students to be recognized, but chafed at the realization that this work was considered so out of the ordinary as to deserve comment, or that others mistakenly perceived that their students were somehow more special than the young people they themselves worked with or knew or heard about.

And it did not take long for the students to understand the darker side of the adult amazement in their researcher identities, both during their research trips in Los Angeles and in Sacramento—the belief that students should not be asking such pointed questions or could not possibly have the capacity to fully understand the complex issues informing their research. Indeed, this aversion to young people doing research that was anything more than cosmetic, and was in fact critical, was often compounded by the fact that the young researchers in question were students of color. The written reflections at the beginning of this section reveal student after student coming to terms with the fact that some of the adults (and young people) they encountered could not reconcile their researcher and racial identities. Carolina put it bluntly when she said that many people looked at them "as if we didn't belong."

Gustavo reinforced this idea when he noted that people in Beverly Hills looked at his research team "as if we were people from another planet" who "shouldn't be around them." He noted the contrast between how he felt doing research in Beverly Hills and his feelings of increased comfort in the more familiar environs of South Los Angeles. While some of these feelings originated with the students themselves, many of whom had not previously traveled outside of their neighborhoods or interacted with white people outside of their school buildings, both the students and adult mentors knew that the sense of suspicion with which some adults viewed them was more than a product of their own discomfort. Adult mentors frequently had to explain what the students were doing when they took students to more affluent areas in Los Angeles—justifications that were not needed when students were collecting data in their own communities.

This clash between students' identities as researchers and their identities as young people of color living in low-income communities resulted in stress; as Dimitri put it, it could be "nerve wracking." He referenced the strain of feeling "out of place" and "not really fitting in." Importantly, however, he was able to put his personal feelings of discomfort into a larger social context—he noted that while the affluence of Beverly Hills made it a magnet for a variety of tourists, exposing residents to a wide variety of people, his community did not attract visitors. As he asks, "How often do you see a tourist in Watts or South Central?" Franklin made a similar connection between his personal experiences and societal inequality in his reflection; while he starts out describing the differences in educational resources between "urban" and "suburban" communities in the third person, he quickly recognizes his membership in the urban community and begins using the collective pronoun—"rich schools ask for less while *we* ask for more, but yet *we* still do not get any resources."

The critical nature of YPAR, and particularly the fact that it engages young people in sophisticated social analysis while they are in an especially crucial phase of their civic identity development, makes it virtually inevitable that stressful situations will emerge that cause students to question themselves and their place in society. This stress can feel dangerous to adult mentors attempting to help navigate students through this process because it could lead to anger, sadness, resignation—all feelings that caregivers and educators want to spare their young mentees. And it is not a stress that will necessarily ease as the research process continues—as we will discuss in the next chapter, students' findings oftentimes confirm what they already know viscerally, confirming the fact that they, their families, and their peers are receiving fewer educational resources than they deserve and that other residents of their city and country enjoy, and that they are attempting to succeed in a system that seems stacked against them.

The fear of academic and/or civic alienation is a real one for adults who facilitate YPAR programs, and one that the adult mentors in the Council were constantly aware of and attempting to mitigate. They communicated to students that the most important aspect of the research experience was not necessarily inspiring immediate change or redress of problems that they had learned through their work were extremely deep-seated in society, but their personal development as researchers and youth leaders who could demonstrate the power and authority of youth voice and contribute to a movement greater than themselves for educational and social justice.

Students internalized this message quickly. Just as Franklin recognized the injustice inherent in the fact that he and his classmates begged for more educational resources while their more affluent peers enjoyed more than they knew what to do with, he also noted that it could be a source of investigation as well as sadness. "That question was so powerful to me," he wrote. Similarly, Gustavo channeled his frustration over feeling unwelcome in Beverly Hills into a call for action for himself and his peers, writing that it was "our turn to go and fight for our rights to a better education." This sense of empowerment in the face of inequality is one of the goals of YPAR.

References

Alvermann, D. E. (2006). Struggling adolescent readers: A cultural construction. In A. McKeough, L. M. Phillips, V. Timmons, & J. L. Lupart (Eds.), *Understanding literacy development: A global view* (pp. 95–111). Mahwah, NJ: Erlbaum.

Faggella-Luby, M., Ware, S., & Capozzoli, A. (2009). Adolescent literacy—reviewing adolescent literacy reports: Key components and critical questions. *Journal of Literacy Research, 41*, 453–475.

Gagnon, P. (2003). *Educating democracy: State standards to ensure a civic core.* Washington, D.C. Albert Shanker Institute.

International Reading Association & National Council of Teachers of English. (1996). *Standards for the English Language Arts.* Newark, DE: International Reading Association.

National Center for Education Statistics. (2014, May 7). *The nation's report card: 2013 mathematics and reading grade 12 assessments.* Retrieved from: http://nces.ed.gov/nationsreportcard/subject/publications/main2013/pdf/2014087.pdf

National Governors Association. (2010). *Common Core state standards for English Language Arts & Literacy in History/Social Studies.* Washington, DC.

Paris, D., & Ball, A. (2009). Teacher knowledge in culturally and linguistically complex classrooms: Lessons from the golden age and beyond. In L.M. Morrow, R. Rueda, & D. Lapp (Eds.), *Handbook of research on literacy instruction: Issues of diversity, policy, and equity* (pp. 379–395). New York: Guilford.

Torney-Purta, J., Barber, C., & Richardson, W. (2005). *How teachers' preparation relates to students' civic knowledge and engagement in the United States: Analysis from the IEA Civic Education Study.* Boston, MA: Center for Information and Research on Civic Learning and Engagement.

Torney-Purta, J., & Vermeer, S. (2004). *Developing citizenship competencies from kindergarten through grade 12: A background paper for policymakers and educators.* Denver: Education Commission of the States.

Watts, R., & Flanagan, C. (2007). Pushing the envelope on civic engagement: A developmental and liberation psychology perspective. *The Journal of Community Psychology, 35*, 779–792.

FIGURE 13 The Council family celebrates after their presentation at the 2011 Annual Meeting of the American Educational Research Association

FIGURE 14 Ernest addresses the audience at the 2010 summer seminar presentation

INTERLUDE

Changing Young Lives in the Council

In this interlude, Nicole talks to Laurence Tan, the longest-serving teacher in the Council, and to some of the students he mentored during the 2010–2011 school year. Karina Arias, Cesar Ramirez, Frank Reed, and Miguel Sosa discuss what they've learned through their involvement with the Council and the influence that it continues to have on their lives.

Nicole: How do you think that the Council was similar to traditional school, and what do you think made it different?

Karina: When our group first started working together, we had a hard time connecting, so we really looked toward the teachers. We looked toward them to tell us what to do at first. But what was different and what challenged me was that it wasn't like that in the Council. We looked to others to tell us what to do at first because we're so used to that in school. You have to do your homework like this, you have to write your sentences like this, you have to write this essay about this topic. But the Council was different because those leaders that we looked up to gave us the power to switch it up and do whatever we wanted, but also were there to provide the structure as to what would work best in order to help us grow and help us teach each other. So we were looking for leadership, but those leaders helped us become leaders ourselves—that's what was different, and that's what was challenging. That's what made us grow and become the team that we were.

Nicole: What did you learn through the Council?

Cesar: My experience with the Council has taught me to be more open-minded. It's hard to explain, but it's taught me ways to understand what is right and wrong and what's really going on in my community—stuff that I never knew. There were injustices repeating themselves. The theory and the vocabulary that we learned in the Council gave me information that helped me understand my life. It impacted me because it showed me that I could make a difference in problems in my community. It was different from the schools that I attended.

Laurence: As a teacher, this is the kind of stuff that I would love to do 24/7 with my students, you know what I mean? This kind of work. But as a teacher it's hard, and we end up doing it outside of the regular day. When you ask about doing stuff that people aren't ready for or aren't used to, I think it's necessary to have alternative spaces like this even though we want to normalize it and it should be in schools.

Frank: I think it opened up my eyes to "the real," I guess you could say. You start to see how things really are when you do the research that we did. You learn that things aren't as good as you might think they are, but that through research you can speak up against that. That is really important because if more people can speak up against that, then maybe we can do something about it.

Nicole: Which parts of the research process did you like best?

Cesar: The part of data collection and fieldwork that had the most impact on me was when we went to see the different districts and the different schools. We'd look at them on the map and see the demographics, how they change from Beverly Hills High to Manual Arts High. We'd see the differences, and we would literally interview these students—we'd ask the students at Beverly Hills the same questions we'd ask at Manual Arts, and we'd see that they have similar problems to us and different problems from us. They'd have thousands of computers when we had five, and those had software on them from 2004. We were reminded that they were getting something that we weren't and we were figuring out why—why they were so fortunate and we weren't.

Miguel: To me, the most interesting part of the process was the exposure to inequality. That's what separates the Council from traditional schooling. At school they just kind of *tell* you, but the Council *proves* it to you and makes you want to do something. Giving you a voice makes you want to do something about it.

Karina: My favorite part is always the survey. I think I'm just more numbers-oriented. I like collecting numbers and seeing percentages and seeing how one thing outweighs the other.

Frank: I agree with Karina. I like when you go out and see that one person thinks this way, and then you think another person is going to think the same way but they have a totally different perspective. I always think that's really interesting. The whole idea of being out interacting with other people instead of being trapped in a classroom, that's really good. Being able to go out and ask people what they really feel about something and getting an outcome.

Nicole: What does it feel like to present in front of an audience of researchers and policymakers and teachers and community members? How does it make you feel to show them what you've found?

Frank: The presentation at the UCLA Labor Center was a little easier because there wasn't as big of a crowd. It was a lot of work, but it helped us get ready for AERA. We bonded and we came together as one. When we got to AERA, we showed that we really did bond because we were on point. Throughout the whole process of getting the research done, you get to bond with other people—get to know their perspectives and get to know them—and it makes the whole outcome better.

Cesar: It was amazing! I would get, like, a rush to know that you're educating the people who should be educating you. You're checking these people and letting them know what they shouldn't be doing. I think the most powerful thing that we did was cut out the whole recommendation part we were given and say instead that we're giving demands. It was a powerful experience, especially in New Orleans, where we knew what we were saying and we had a powerful crew. If we missed anything, we knew we had someone to back us up. We were there to let people know and speak our minds about what is going on, and instead of just asking, what are you going to do, we gave them information about the best ways to change what was going on.

Miguel: It was nerve-wracking because you had that adrenaline rush and you're scared that your voice is going to crack and that no one will care about what you have to say, but then you realize that you do have a voice and that people are listening to you. You're educating them. Most high school students don't feel like they have that voice. Presenting at these conferences makes you feel more confident and like you're ready to question everything.

Karina: I think I was 16 or 17 when I was in front of educators and policymakers, and I wasn't satisfied with the education system. Miguel and Cesar talked about how we overcame our obstacles and talked to these policymakers, telling them what we were not satisfied with, telling them what needs to be changed. I feel like a lot of them did listen. A lot of them did want to change things, but sometimes you still feel like it takes more than one presentation to do that.

I want to talk more about how the group ourselves, we supported each other. We cared about each other. We made each other proud, we made [Laurence] Tan proud, we made Nicole proud—we made everybody proud. We were passionate about this. I came out of those presentations very satisfied. I came out of those presentations even stronger than I was when I went in.

Nicole: How do you think you are different today than you would have been if you had never been in the Council?

Cesar: It literally opened my eyes to everything that I do and see now. It gave me a sense of critical thinking. I didn't know what thinking really was. The Council showed me how to analyze something—what caused it, what are the effects, how can we change it, what are the options. The way I see the world now is so different. Yeah, I have problems of my own, but if I can help somebody just a little bit with these bigger problems, it makes me feel better and feel successful.

Miguel: The Council has shaped who I am now. It's changed my mindset so now I'm always thinking about helping others. I can't settle for less—I'm constantly climbing up ladders and looking for something more to give back to the community and help the schools. The Council has also helped me deal with adversity. If it wasn't for the Council, I probably would have taken the easy way out and I never would have gotten the GPA that I got. It has shaped the way that I think and the way that I deal with things.

Karina: When I first started 9th grade, all I cared about was getting straight A's and playing softball. In 10th grade is when I realized that I cared about helping the community as well, and I also started realizing that there were many differences. That's when I knew that I wanted to become an educator as well because I felt the impact that all of you in the whole group had on me. That's when I knew I wanted to inspire others in the same way that they inspired me and study sociology and education. Those years are when I was pushed to think outside the box and challenge authority.

Frank: The Council impacted me early. After my first week with the group, I would go to class and tell my teacher, you're trying to put me at the bottom of the social hierarchy. It made me feel like there were things I needed to speak up against and encourage others to speak up against. It opened my mind up to injustices that are happening that people don't realize. I used to just think I could just "do me," but now I know I have to do things to better myself so that I can better my community.

FIGURE 15 Council members circle up and do a unity clap before their spring 2011 presentation at the UCLA Labor Center in Los Angeles

7

PRODUCING AND SHARING RESEARCH

"My name is Dimitri, and I am a junior at Locke High School. We are the Council of Youth Research. The Council is a critical space that I believe should be offered to all youth all over the world. This space allows youth to engage with adults and have intellectual conversations as if it was a common thing to do. When we gather together, to me it feels like a family reunion. But when I think about it, why aren't places like the Council of Youth Research commonly found? Places like the Council of Youth Research should be created because it is important for youth to develop their critical consciousness and be the intellectuals that they really are. So I challenge all of you to pay attention to our presentations. And like Gandhi said, 'Be the change that you want to see in the world.'"

"My name is Katie Briggs. As an educator, it's not very often that we get to say that our students get to teach us. And I think the Council of Youth Research is my time and space to stop, listen, and think about how to best learn and how to best teach. That's what I think the Council means to me. But it also teaches me a level of accountability. It makes me realize that these young people are expecting greatness from me, as I should expect from them. I think you'll experience that today."

"Good afternoon, everyone. My name is Emily. I am a senior at Crenshaw High School and a member of the UCLA Council of Youth Research. I have learned and experienced so many things through this program. I have gone out and explored things that I never dreamed of exploring. Going out and exploring with IDEA helped me develop into an autonomous leader, and gave me the skills to not only be educated, but to be able to educate others. In presenting with the Council, I also strengthened my leadership skills and public speaking skills. And it also inspired me to do more—to look beyond my horizons. I am currently the secretary of my School Site Council, and I will be attending a four-year university in the fall."

"*My name is Eduardo Lopez, but call me Eddie. I teach at Roosevelt High School in Boyle Heights in East Los Angeles. I've been teaching for six years, but working with the Council for two years. I used to be an educator who was conscious of educational inequities and discussed them in the classroom but then didn't know what to do. So the Council, for me as an educator, has meant giving me the tools to actually start bringing change and becoming a transformative educator. I just want to end with this little quote that I think is fitting for this occasion. It's by Victor Hugo. About education, he once said, 'He or she who opens a school door closes a prison.' I very much believe that, and I think as educators, we need to start thinking beyond the classroom to the implications that our profession has on the broader society.*"

"*My name is Ebony Cain, and 10 years ago I was a student in the Council. Now I'm a doctoral student working with the Council. What the Council means to me is an opportunity to go home, to see the place where you have people support you, a place where people will help you grow. The Council transformed me. It changed me from a person who had no hopes of going to college to someone who's now a doctoral student who gets to see students change their schools and people's lives every day.*"

One by one, each of these five Council members stepped forward to talk about the impact that the program had on them as their peers stood on either side of the hotel ballroom silently supporting them. An audience of nearly 100 people looked on. Their testimonials kicked off a 90-minute session at the 2011 Annual Meeting of the American Educational Research Association in New Orleans, Louisiana, during which the students presented the results of the research they had spent over nine months planning, conducting, and analyzing. For many, this trip represented their first opportunity to visit a city outside of California, or even Los Angeles. For all, it was a symbolic moment—the public sharing of a personal, academic, and civic journey and an opportunity to demonstrate the power of youth voice to an audience drawn from the largest professional organization of educational researchers in North America.

This chapter will detail the importance of public research presentations as crucial components of YPAR practice, both as opportunities to share the knowledge created by students with family, teachers, policymakers, and community members and as celebrations of students' developing identities as scholars and researchers. We will explain two ways in which the Council conceived of and planned presentations differently from the way they are often created. First, instead of viewing presentations as culminating events signaling the conclusion of the research process, the Council saw them as a part of the continuous cycle of praxis—a signal post, important but temporary, as students and teachers moved from action to reflection and back again. Second, while presentations are often seen as outward-facing and geared primarily toward impacting audience members to think or do something, the Council kept the focus squarely on the students during these events, carefully choreographing them to reinforce students' confidence and pride in their work and viewing audience impact as an important, but secondary, concern.

We will begin by exploring the careful and purposeful planning process that went into determining the locations, audience compositions, and formats of Council student presentations. We will then move on to an analysis of the performative nature of these presentations before zeroing in on the impact they had on Council members and those who witnessed their presentations. We will conclude by describing the ways that presentations were situated within the praxis of the Council and the next steps that took place after presentations had ended.

Presentations as Celebratory Rites of Passage

Planning for Presentations

In Chapter 3, we explored the concept of communities of practice as a crucial element of YPAR. Students engage in legitimate peripheral participation in a purposeful collaborative that leads them on a journey of apprenticeship toward mastery. This is a fitting way to describe the process that young people went through during their time in the Council. Students apprenticed themselves to adult (and more experienced youth) researchers, learning the tools of the trade throughout the summer and school year, and at the conclusion of a research cycle, when students were prepared to share the knowledge they had created, presentations represented symbolic turning points when they became full members of the community.

In a more practical sense, presentations offer provisional end points for a research experience that, in reality, stretches on far past any arbitrary day or time. Adults chose dates that served as deadlines to motivate and challenge students to ask themselves what they had found to a certain point and share their results. During the 2010–2011 school year, students had three opportunities to present their research—once at the conclusion of the summer seminar, once at a spring community forum in Los Angeles, and once at the AERA Annual Meeting. Each of these presentations involved careful planning on the part of the Council adults in order to support students at different stages of their research as they shared their findings with distinct audiences.

Students' first opportunity for public presentation of research was on August 6, 2010, as the culmination of the summer seminar. The adults in the Council knew that the overarching theme of the summer work—reflecting on the 10 years since the filing of *Williams v. California*—demanded the attention of politicians, policymakers, and other community leaders who worked within an educational context shaped by this case. As a result, they wanted the student presentations to take place at a venue that would grab the attention of these stakeholders and encourage them to attend.

John and Ernest had developed a relationship with the office of then–Los Angeles mayor Antonio Villaraigosa over the years that had led to support for the Council's work in the form of student summer jobs. They leveraged this relationship to arrange for the students' summer presentation to take place in the Tom Bradley Room on the top floor of Los Angeles City Hall—a beautiful space with high ceilings, ornate decorations, and 360-degree views of the city. None of the Council members, student or adult, had ever visited this room before the day of the presentation, and the looks on their faces as they walked in for the first time and realized that they would be speaking there spoke volumes. This intentional choice of venue represented a message to students—that the importance of their voices necessitated a room of sufficient grandeur to hold them.

Nicole sent personal invitations to the Mayor, all members of the City Council and Board of Education, and the state assembly members who served students' districts, in addition to administrators from students' schools and all community members who had been interviewed or otherwise participated in their research. Whenever any of these high-profile city leaders attended a student presentation, the Council adults usually offered them a few minutes to introduce themselves and comment on the student research. While these opportunities allowed politicians to connect with some of their potential constituents, the more important impacts involved boosts in students' self-concept and increased awareness of powerful student voice.

This combination of leveraging resources and making intentional statements about the value of student work through the choice of venues was a constant for Council adults as they planned for further student presentations. The summer presentation took place on a Friday morning—a choice made not only to coincide with and commemorate the final day of the seminar, but also to accommodate the schedules of the educational and political invitees. One consequence of this time choice was that many of the students' family members could not attend due to work or other commitments. As a result, the adults planned the spring research presentation for a Saturday morning at a location that involved far less red tape than City Hall.

John again leveraged his connections within UCLA to secure the UCLA Labor Center as the venue, which was a community- and labor-friendly space in a central city location. While invitations were again extended to city leaders, the focus during this gathering, which served as a dress rehearsal for the AERA presentation in New Orleans, was more geared toward offering friends, families, and educators the opportunity to learn about the work their students had been engaging in all school year. Translation services were provided that (in addition to student code-switching during their presentations) helped Spanish-speaking family members fully participate in the experience.

Structure of the Presentations

Both presentations followed a similar format. Ernest and John welcomed the audience and provided some background about the history and practice of youth research before turning the floor over to the five student teams, who would offer 10–15-minute presentations with the help of PowerPoint and then play 3–5-minute documentary films that they had created to dramatize their research topics. While the summer presentation featured mixed-school teams, the logistical challenges of meeting during the school year and finding time for data collection and analysis made it more appropriate for the spring presentation to highlight school teams.

The structure of the presentations mirrored the students' research process. They began with explanations of the pressing problems they observed in their school communities and how they developed researchable questions based on their concerns. They continued by referencing the major theorists they turned to in order to better understand their topics, distilling dense philosophical texts into accessible summaries. Discussions of methodology and data collection tools followed, which provided the launching pad for students to offer the claims and evidence that they had developed as a result of their investigations. Always aware of the need to triangulate their data, students presented a combination of survey results, interview quotes, and observational field notes in order to back up every claim.

Since the presentations generally followed the structure of academic articles, the logical way to conclude would have been to offer recommendations for addressing the problems based on the findings. The Council altered this formula; in order to highlight the fact that this research was not occurring in a lab but in the very communities in which they lived, students decided to emphasize the urgency of tackling these problems by concluding with "demands." Students were prepared to think about the various stakeholders in the audience—parents, teachers, administrators, district officials, politicians—and crafted marching orders toward each of these constituencies. They looked into the audience, locking eyes with individuals, and told them what they could do the next day to start solving these problems.

This concept of "demands" was a crucial aspect of the student presentations because it jolted audience members into remembering that the student presenters were not consultants or researchers with purely academic interests in improving urban schools; instead, they were students who were living the troubling conditions that they were sharing. While audience members usually started out being very impressed by the students and their skills, the demands were an opportunity to remind them that these students were speaking on behalf of hundreds, if not thousands, of their peers in an attempt to secure equitable educational opportunities for them and future generations of students.

In Los Angeles, these audience members consisted largely of classroom educators, administrators, and community members. A very different audience greeted the students when they presented their work at AERA; this time, the students were talking to university professors, graduate students, and educational researchers. The adults started writing proposals to bring Council students to this conference the year prior and have continued to bring students to this conference each year since. (See Appendix D for the AERA proposal submitted for this conference.) Professors, graduate students, and teachers associated with the Council have also featured students as presenters at meetings of the National Council of Teachers of English and the Digital Media and Learning Hub.

The adult members of the Council found it important to share the Council's work at academic conferences as well as in local community spaces in order to highlight the innovative contributions that the Council model was making to theory, research, and practice in the areas of critical pedagogy, critical and digital literacy, civic engagement, and YPAR itself. Just as the YPAR research in which the students engaged aimed to inject the voices of young people into decision making at the school and community level, so did the YPAR research in which the adults engaged aim to transform educational conferences into places where young people could share their perspectives instead of merely being talked *about*.

Nicole and Antero heard Ernest remind the adults during every planning meeting that while the group could easily spend all of its time engaged in program implementation to keep the Council running, the need to write about this work and share the lessons learned with the broader scholarly community in order to re-imagine the who, what, when, why, and how of educational research remained just as crucial. We will explore the rewards and challenges involved in engaging in YPAR in the academy further in Chapter 8.

Since the AERA audience came to the students' session interested not only in the content of their research, but also in its guiding theories and methodologies, this presentation featured a unique structure. As we shared at the start of this chapter, the presentation began with short testimonials from various Council representatives, followed by a short explanation of the Council's origins and composition provided by Nicole. At this point, the 10-minute student presentations began, interspersed with commentary given by the teachers and graduate students about the ways that the Council sought to redefine traditional notions of research, literacy, and democracy.

Since the graduate students were working on developing academic articles about the relationship of YPAR to each of these concepts, they shared their research questions with the audience just as the students did. These included:

Research Questions about Research

1. How does the Council of Youth Research help us think differently about what is possible in educational research through the inclusion of youth perspectives?
2. What have we learned from our work with the Council about the nature of Youth Participatory Action Research (YPAR)?
3. How does the process of incorporating youth voice have an impact on youth themselves and their agency in school reform?

Research Questions about Literacy

1. What does critical literacy look like in practice with young people? How does practice help us understand what critical literacy is?
2. What are the connections between critical literacy practice and civic engagement practice with young people?
3. What are the pedagogies that enable critical literacy?

Research Questions about Democracy

1. What vision of democracy should schools provide students with?
2. What sorts of learning opportunities empower students to become civic agents?
3. How does the Council embody a critical democratic practice?

As Nicole organized the flow of the presentation, she consciously chose to position these research questions before or after specific student presentations that seemed to embody relevant ideas so that the adults could call the audience's attention to particular choices that the students made in their work.

While the PowerPoint presentations that the student groups shared generally adhered to the topics of teaching, curriculum, resources, social/physical ecology, and leadership, the films that they shared took a different direction. The videos that the students made during the summer seminar often stretched to five minutes or more—a length that would have been prohibitive during a jam-packed 90-minute AERA session. As a result, students created shorter films in the style of public service announcements for this presentation that focused on the transformative experience of the Council more so than the content of the research.

Before exploring these videos and what they revealed about the impact of the Council on students' academic skills, civic identity, and self-concept, we turn to some of the performative moves that Council students made to engage audience members during their presentations—choices that revealed the unique styles that each group brought to YPAR.

Presentations as Performance

As we discussed in Chapter 5, student groups often chose to deviate from more popular forms of data collection (surveys, interviews, focus groups) as they developed more comfort with the research process itself, branching off into spoken word or personal reflection based on the interests and abilities of the students and their team leaders. The same phenomenon occurred during presentations as Council students loosened up and began to play off their personalities and their unique strengths as public speakers. As a result, Council presentations morphed from relatively traditional research presentations into engaging performances grounded in students' identities as young people.

Students felt especially welcome to experiment with alternative speaking styles during a second presentation that they gave at AERA. In addition to the 90-minute presentation that they had all to themselves, the Council members were part of another presentation that featured several other YPAR groups from across the country, featuring students from Oakland and New York City. Adults from these groups collaborated to introduce more youth voice into the conference through a two-hour-long morning session that operated more as a roundtable or research festival. Each group of young people commandeered a corner of a large hotel ballroom and had the opportunity to speak with more intimate gatherings of audience members who would rotate between presentations every 15 minutes or come and go as they pleased.

This format demanded more flexibility and creativity from the students since they could not simply proceed through their prearranged set of slides; instead, they were pushed to interact with audience members to keep their attention in a stimulus-rich environment. Students rose to the challenge in a variety of ways that spoke to their particular talents. For instance, consider how Cesar strove to make the dense musings of early 20th-century philosopher Antonio Gramsci relatable to himself, his peers, and the audience:

> I use Gramsci in my daily life by being counter-hegemonic and educating my community. For example, I have a friend who was being oppressed, who thinks that school sucks and his education sucks. He thinks that money is what succeeding is. So I questioned him to get him critically thinking and explain that the dominant class is doing this to him for a reason—to make sure that he stays in the hood.
>
> So this made me question myself about why people are thinking this way in my community, which led me to doing research and finding out not only why they think this way, but how I can help them to stop thinking this way. As you have seen, as organic intellectuals we have given you this marvelous example of how we use Gramsci in our daily lives. But our goal is not only to show you this, but to make sure we create places where organic and traditional intellectuals can learn from one another as a *familia*, as a family and as a unit.
>
> So now I wanted to interact with everyone and ask you guys a question. Out of our presentation, and examples we gave you, how are you guys being counter-hegemonic or how can you be counter-hegemonic?

In this case, Cesar decided to forsake the more formal data he had collected during the summer and school year and demonstrate to audience members how theory matters even when folks are engaged in personal conversations with friends and loved ones. This style fit Cesar's personality well—he was always the student who strove to make connections between what he was learning in more academic spaces and the messages being transmitted by popular culture and community members.

Admittedly, the adults who were listening to Cesar were taken aback and slow to answer his question at first; after all, they were accustomed to presentations that required nothing more than passive listening from audience members. After a brief pause, however, audience members began sharing the contexts in which they taught or researched and exploring ways in which they could challenge status quo ideas about youth voice in their work with students.

The group from Roosevelt High School also engaged with narratives promulgated by popular culture about young people in order to get audience members' attention, focusing on a documentary film that openly criticized their school by name. Davis Guggenheim's film *Waiting for Superman* (2010), which explored the troubled American public school system, followed the educational trajectories of several young people around the country. In one scene, the narrator ominously wonders what will happen to a bright young girl if she is forced to go to her neighborhood high school—Roosevelt—since it has such a low graduation rate. The only message that viewers would take away from the film about Roosevelt was that it was "one of the worst performing high schools in Los Angeles."

Dressed in matching Superman t-shirts, the Roosevelt group showed a clip from the film and then provided their own counter-stories to illuminate the many other facets of their school community. Maggie addressed the audience:

> As you can see, oppression causes people to not realize their own superpowers. It leads us to believe that we do not have the power in ourselves to change the oppression that has been placed on us.
>
> Oppression also negatively frames our communities, and many times, these frames are formed from movies such as *Waiting for Superman* and other forms of media. When movies like this call us gangsters, dropouts, and failures, how do you expect us to react? Let me ask you this—if this is the only way that the media has portrayed us, how would you look at us? How would you see us?

Squirming a bit in their seats, audience members raised their hands and admitted that without the context that the students were providing, they would likely possess overwhelmingly negative views about the teachers and students at Roosevelt High School. Instead of making assumptions that academically struggling schools are simply failures, the students pushed audience members to consider the ways that oppressive educational and community structures could bend, but not break, a vitally important community institution.

Students from Manual Arts High School used the intimate setting of the roundtable presentation to tell audience members about how they had used their research as a springboard for developing professional development sessions for teachers at their school. The more they discovered about the kinds of powerful curriculum to which all students were entitled, the more they realized that they could be agents of change by educating their teachers about what they needed and wanted from them. Patricia explained the process:

As we presented, we used professional language so that the teachers would take us seriously. Also, during our facilitation of group work, we demonstrated skills that the teachers could use in the future. We gave them immediate feedback. We repeated classroom norms such as, "No one of us is as smart as all of us." And each group member had a specific role so that there was no passive learning, therefore helping the teachers understand the necessary processes they need to know in order to teach this kind of lesson in their classrooms.

As Patricia spoke, the faces of audience members registered surprise—surprise (and perhaps disbelief) that young people could possess knowledge that could improve teacher practice. This group reminded those who had come to simply hear a presentation that presentations should be the beginning of further change rather than ends in themselves. These young people did not engage in YPAR simply to shout their findings into a void; instead, they had come to build knowledge that could be shared with others to create lasting change. It was a logical extension of the "marching orders" that students gave as they concluded their formal presentations.

Anecdotally, we know that many people who came to Council presentations that year in Los Angeles or New Orleans were tremendously moved by the students' work—it was not uncommon to see tears standing in people's eyes as the presentations concluded. Dozens of individuals would approach the students and adults after these events and talk about the YPAR groups they planned on starting, or the new instructional practices they planned to implement in their classrooms, or simply the reflection they engaged in about how they perceived youth voice and the role that young people could play in educational reform efforts.

Melanie Bertrand, one of the graduate students who worked with the Council during the 2010–2011 school year, labeled such audience responses "promoting" in an article that was published in *Educational Administration Quarterly* in 2014 because they invited reciprocal dialogue between students and adult decision makers in which the ideas of both parties were respected and honored as useful. We witnessed many examples of promoting responses to the Council's work that year, including concrete policy changes that principals made to their schools in response to the students' research.

Unfortunately, Melanie noted in her article that the majority of responses that adult decision makers had to the Council's work could better be characterized as "inhibiting" because, while they appeared to praise the students' work, they failed to take it seriously or consider young people as potential partners in the work of school reform. This failure usually took the form of adults being surprised that teenagers possessed the capacity to conduct research at all, and then proceeding to discredit the research as lacking the rigor to meaningfully contribute to addressing educational challenges. We definitely experienced responses that seemed to minimize the student performances by characterizing them as "cute" or as mere academic exercises that had no relevancy in the world beyond the classroom.

Nevertheless, as we have maintained throughout this book, the Council always put exponentially more focus on empowering young people rather than pushing for any particular policy changes. Martin Luther King Jr. famously stated that "the arc of the moral universe is long, but it bends toward justice." The theory of change that the Council espoused involved providing critical and transformative educational experiences to teachers and young people who would respectively teach and become the next generation of leaders. Small victories along the way provided hope, but the goal was much larger than change in any one school or school district. And through this lens, student responses to the Council demonstrated that the Council could claim success.

Impact of Presentations on Student Identity, Achievement, and Practice

Strains of music begin to play as the camera focuses in on a black background with white lettering: "The Locke High School Council of Youth Researchers want to know . . ." The video then cuts to Cesar's face as he asks, "How do we build organic leadership?" We then hear an adult explaining that leadership is not something that can be developed, but instead is "something you're born with." Red letters emerge onto the screen as the adult talks that ask incredulously, "Born that way?"

As mentioned previously, the videos that Council students produced for their AERA presentation highlighted how the group impacted them as individuals, students, and citizens. The films illustrated student growth in two ways. First, analysis of the structures of the videos implicitly demonstrated the academic skills that students mastered in order to tell visual stories that complemented and extended their research. Second, analysis of what students say in the videos offered an explicit window into the Council's impact on their personal and civic identity development. In this section, we will focus on the video that the Locke High School group produced and explore what this text revealed about the Council's influence.

From the very beginning of the Locke group's video, which strove to identify leadership as a skill that develops organically through community, collaboration, and caring, we can see evidence that students are presenting an argument and then seeking to address and discredit counterarguments—skills that are at the core of powerful and effective persuasive writing. The students offer and then dismiss the idea that leaders are born rather than made through the combination of a quote and strategically placed text questioning that quote.

The video continues with clips of several educators continuing to promulgate the idea that only adults can be leaders; one adult explains that his job is to "seep knowledge into the brain stems" of young people, who are expected to be followers. Again, students indicate that they are about to present a counter argument by flashing the word "Really??!" on the screen. At this point, Miguel, another student in the group, appears. He points at the camera and asks, "Aren't you tired of people telling you that you can't be a leader?"

At this point, the tone of the video shifts (accompanied by a change in music). Instead of seeing adults, we now see young members of the Council looking directly into the camera and explaining the ways that they are leaders in their schools and communities. The students consciously made the choice to present the arguments of their opposition and then deconstruct them with the evidence of their own personal experience. Each of the testimonials is accompanied by still photographs of the students in school and community spaces embodying what it means to them to be leaders. Watching the students speak, we are struck by the ways in which students are taking seriously their identities as developing citizens with the responsibility to give back to their communities.

Several of the students talk specifically about the ways that the Council helped them to find their voices and become educated about ways to stand up for their communities. The group was clearly aware of the power of film to appeal to the emotions of their audience members in order to persuade them, because at one point, as Miguel is talking about how the Council has impacted him, a picture of his cherubic, smiling little brother appears on the screen. Miguel explains, "What I've noticed is that since he's seen me doing extra activities, he kind of follows me around. He wants to get more involved. The thing that touched me the other day is that he actually told me that he wants to be like me one day."

After the students present their evidence that leaders can be developed and that young people can be leaders, they turn to their concluding statement, which urges others to action. Gustavo yells, "Impact takes time, courage, and unity. So how are you contributing to the impact?" The screen goes black and the message appears: "Demand leadership from yourself and work toward impacting others."

Aristotle offered ethos, pathos, and logos as the three foundational means of persuasion. The Locke group's video demonstrated all three types, but in ways that expanded their meanings by incorporating youth voice. In terms of ethos, or appealing to credibility to make a powerful argument, the Council students utilized the language and tools of research in order to position themselves as experts. While they used the tools of the academy, they simultaneously transformed the tools because of their identities as young people declaring that they had the right to produce and share new knowledge.

In terms of pathos, or appealing to emotion, the students demonstrated a sophisticated ability to use their youth in order to draw audience members in and then surprise viewers by demanding that they be taken seriously as more than "just kids."

And in terms of logos, or appealing to reasoning, the students used triangulation in order to bolster their arguments, offering several quotes, images, or pieces of data in order to support each point they made so that their points could not simply be written off as personal opinions. Importantly, however, their work strove to open up the research process enough so that personal experience could be considered valid and persuasive data.

We could have performed a similar analysis of all of the Council groups' videos and presented many more stories about the ways we have seen young people blossom as a result of the learning opportunities offered by the Council. But we will encapsulate them all through Cesar's reflection on the AERA presentation, which highlights the ways in which critical work that takes seriously the agency, ability, and genius of young people has the power to transform lives:

> The trip to New Orleans was an experience that changes a person. I never thought I could be such a revolutionary, but an experience like AERA tells me that I have a future in this field. It tells me that I am not someone that will sit around and take oppression; I am someone who will be an advocate for change. After listening to educators and administrators applaud us on our work, I realized that I can make a change.

Praxis: After the Presentations Have Ended

In *Pedagogy of the Oppressed*, Paulo Freire (1970) defined "praxis" as "reflection and action directed at the structures to be transformed" (p. 126). This cyclical process does not have a fixed end point or any arbitrary markers of success or failure; instead, it represents a continuous journey toward liberation and justice. The work of the Council of Youth Research did not end after presentations concluded. Presentations offered opportunities for celebration and gratitude that jump-started the next cycle of planning, implementation, and further reflection.

While the end of the 2010–2011 school year did not mark the end of the Council's work, it did mark the end of the foundation funding that had allowed us to engage with YPAR on such a large scale. While much of the team realized that the opportunities and resources to travel up and down the state of California and across the country with 30 high school students, 5 teachers, and 10 university educators was one-of-a-kind and could not last forever, they remained steadfast in the belief that they were worth every penny and led to transformations in students' lives and in theory, research, and practice.

While subsequent iterations of the Council operated on a much smaller scale in terms of travel to conferences, resources for student transportation and technology, and general logistics, the research continued. It continued as the younger brothers and sisters of Council members joined the group. It continued as some teachers moved on and other teachers came on board. It continued as Ernest moved to New York and the graduate students landed jobs across the country.

It continued because the Council model fundamentally changed the philosophies of teaching and learning of nearly everyone who came in contact with it.

We consider the Council a family, and while it may no longer resemble the robust organization that we enjoyed during the 2010–2011 school year, it is still thriving because it is about the people and the process rather than any particular place or presentation. Our family members have extended the YPAR work in ways we never could have imagined.

Through his involvement in the Council, Laurence realized that students of all grade levels needed to experience this kind of teaching and learning; as a result, he founded a youth organization called the Watts Youth Collective that engages youth in YPAR work from elementary school through college.

D'Artagnan and Eddie recognized the power of YPAR as an educational strategy that could help empower young men of color who were often struggling within the traditional school system and established leadership classes based on the Council's model—D'Artagnan with African-American youth in Inglewood through the Social Justice Learning Institute, and Eddie with Latino youth in Boyle Heights through Compadres Unidos.

While organizing professional development sessions for teachers at Manual Arts High School brought Katie and Antero some satisfaction, they wanted more. They imagined an entire school organized to offer hundreds of students the love and learning experiences that the Council could offer to only 30 students per year. Along with their colleagues, they submitted an application to start a pilot school in the Los Angeles Unified School District. Augustus Hawkins High School opened in the fall of 2012 and continues to follow the dream inspired by the Council.

And the praxis continues. The young people who participated in the Council continue to proceed through college and choose careers. The teachers continue to educate their students toward critical understandings of self and society. And the professors and graduate students continue to engage in YPAR and share this work with the academic community.

We find it fitting to close this chapter with the words that concluded the Council's AERA presentation. The seniors who were about to head off to college stood shoulder to shoulder before the audience and each one gave a final thought that reinforced the power and love that comes from doing and sharing YPAR:

> A—*An idea can change your minds, an idea can transform our lives, and an idea can impact the world. This is why I'm proud to say that I am a member of the UCLA / IDEA Council of Youth Research.*
>
> G—*Growing in this program academically and as a person influences me to inform others, be resistant and make a change.*
>
> E—*Engage all youth in educational research.*
>
> N—*Even though there was a lot of negativity around me—drugs, violence, gangs, and teen pregnancy—I am the youngest in my family and the first to graduate high school and attend a four-year college.*

T—The Youth Council has not only created change in the system, but in the students. It has transformed me and my peers to challenge the dominant systems that oppress me and people like me.

S—Social capital from the community cultural wealth theory has helped me in finding my voice and speaking out about the inequalities in my education by me being a part of my School Site Council.

O—Open your mouths; speak up. Organize programs like the Youth Council. Create a change; make a powerful revolution.

F—Fight against oppression. Fight against inequalities, and fight to get the education that we all deserve.

C—'Cause I am a Latino does not mean that I will end up in the working class. We will keep driving, even through the foggy glass. Change is coming, and best believe it's coming fast.

H—Hope for us students and future generations, like my little sister, lies in powerful curriculum, andragogy, and praxis.

A—For appreciation we all feel for the grad students, teachers, and professors in this room that have helped us to realize that we have nothing to lose but our chains, and transform from conformist to activist.

N—The necessity to make a change to prevent the people from the struggle.

G—Generation. Myka and Shawn, please stand. I pass you guys the torch to continue the change.

E—Eager to continue for change, not just after graduation, but for me to continue it on. And we are . . . AGENTS OF CHANGE!

References

Bertrand, M. (2014). Reciprocal dialogue between educational decision-makers and Students of Color: Opportunities and obstacles. *Educational Administration Quarterly, 50*(5), 812–843.

Freire, P. (1970). *Pedagogy of the oppressed.* New York: Seabury Press.

FIGURE 16 Council students interview Sacramento Mayor Kevin Johnson during the 2010 summer seminar

FIGURE 17 Council students work on their research on the bus trip up to Sacramento during the 2010 summer seminar

INTERLUDE

Demanding Change through YPAR

This final interlude provides the transcript of the speech that Ernest Morrell gave to the audience who attended the Council's presentation at 2011 Annual Meeting of the American Educational Research Association (AERA). Ernest reflects upon what the Council's work means in the context of urban school reform and explains how various educational stakeholders can stand up and make strides in fighting for social justice for all students.

So this is what we do every day in the Council of Youth Research. And I want you to think about that. This is what we do every day in the Council of Youth Research. And I've said this before—to put in context the tragedy of American education, the average student goes to school 180 days a year, and in order to get a high school diploma in the United States, you need to go to school for 13 years. You can do the math; 180 days, 13 years—that is nearly 2500 days of public education. Imagine if this is what happened every day in American education. Imagine that. Because this is the American Educational Research Association, and that's what we get paid to do—to imagine and to make that imagination reality.

I have a series of questions. My job, as session discussant, is to deliver some marching orders to everyone in the room. We tell the students when they speak, "Do not let anyone leave the room without marching orders." This is not enter-tainment—this is engagement. There is a difference. The first question: why isn't this normal academic activity? Why isn't this normal? I love each and every one of these kids, but there is nothing abnormal about them—they don't have three legs, they cannot fly. They are just regular kids who got a chance to par-ticipate in a unique and well-resourced program. There's another 50 million of them in America's schools in need of a similar chance. Why isn't this normal activity? Do not applaud them as exceptional. This is not exceptional work, or at least it shouldn't be if we are doing our jobs in the American Educational Research Association. This is what we're supposed to normalize—make this normal activity, engage students every day, challenge them to develop and to use their voice.

Unless, that is, you don't believe in them. Unless you believe that these are exceptional youth, and the youth that you work with, and the youth in the cities where you do your research are not exceptional. So it's okay that 60 percent of them drop out of school. So it's okay that they finish 9th grade and they cannot read or write. It's okay that you walk by a classroom and see 15 heads on the desk out of 25 students. That's okay if we do not believe in our students.

So my question to the American Educational Research Association is: what do we believe? What do we believe about learning? What do we write about? Sociocultural theory is something that I see in a lot of the manuscripts that I review. But according to sociocultural theory, as I understand it, learning is about engagement. Learning is about participation. Learning is about action. If we believe in learning as participation, what kind of learning do we demand in our classrooms? What kind of learning spaces do we create in our research?

The second question: what do we believe about America's students? Be honest about that. What do we believe about the students in our classrooms and the students in the districts where we teach? Do we believe that the average student can do what these kids just did? That's a question. Do we believe that the average student can do what these kids just did? (Waits for response, some people say, "Yes.") I'll try that again: do we believe that the average student can do what these kids just did? (People shout, "Yes!") Then what the hell are we doing in American education? What are we doing? This is unconscionable. Every kid who drops out is the death of a dream—the dream of that child, the dream of that child's parents and grandparents, neighbors, aunts and uncles, and people who love that child. If we believe in America's students, we have got to do a better job at our job. We have got to find or create reasons for hope. That is what they pay us for at these universities. We get good money, with benefits, and summers to change things, not to make annual pilgrimages to our annual meeting to talk about the problem, but to offer solutions and offer change.

The third question: what do we believe about America's teachers that we stand by and force them to read off of a manuscript to students? My mother, who taught for 42 years, said she never felt so dehumanized as during her last year of teaching. She said her 19-year old granddaughter could do what she was doing, sitting in front of people reading a manuscript. What do we believe? You've seen these (Council) teachers; you've seen what they do. If we believe in America's teachers, and we are the educational leaders—*we are the educational leaders*—we would advocate for them. We would stand by them. We would make it our lives' effort to demonstrate that this kind of pedagogy is what America's teachers are capable of.

Finally: what do we believe about research? Do we believe that because we went to school for 25 years and completed a dissertation that that qualifies us and us only to do research? That only we have an opinion, that only we have values, only we care about education? I can leave Crenshaw High School at 3:30 after I complete my interviews and observations, but Emily and Bernardo—they can't leave because that's their school. So maybe they should be a part of research and not just the objects of research, but the participants in research.

I said finally, but I've got one more: what do we believe about our ability as an organization? Do we believe that we come for four days every April to pontificate on the problems of American education and we have done our job? I published 10 pieces, give me tenure; I published 20 pieces, make me full [professor]; I published 30 pieces, make me God. Is that our role? Or is our role as an organization actually to change the scope of American education? That's what I believe. And that's what they're hoping you believe. And if we believed that, then we would also believe that nothing is inevitable. Nothing is inevitable as long as there is a willingness to contemplate what is happening. Poor kids do not have to receive a poor education in the wealthiest nation in the history of civilization if we believe otherwise. That's what we tell them, right? That you can do whatever it is you want to. We can do whatever it is we set our minds to as an organization. There are 15,000 of us here in New Orleans. That is an army. That is an intellectual army with the force to change American education, if that's what we wanted to do.

So finally—that's the preamble to the marching orders. Marching orders to the students—demand excellence with your excellence. The best form of resistance is to be excellent. You all understand this because you've read Solorzano—conforming makes your enemies happy. Do not make your enemies happy. The way that you resist is by proving them wrong. And if we can't do it, then you've got to do it for us. Your resistance is through excellence.

To the teachers—you have a lot more power than you realize. They say that teaching is the heart of the revolution—you've got to believe that and you have to enact that.

To the graduate students—don't ask small questions for your dissertation even if it makes your committee happy. Big questions. These are big problems—ask big questions. You are the future of American educational research. No small questions. No more rehashing the problem. Intervention. Action. Solution. Engagement. Transformation. Or go home. It's not worth it if you're not going to ask the big questions.

To the adult professional paid researchers, please do what you can to change the nature of this emotionless, negative, passive space that is AERA. You have the power to change this space. You have the power to demand that youth have a voice, that teachers have a voice, that community members have a voice—that we change the scope of research to include participation from multiple communities, that we study intervention. Change this space, because this is what the future of research looks like. And we can do this. We can do this. If you believe that, like these students do, then we will be the change that we want to see.

FIGURE 18 Council students prepare for their interviews in Sacramento in the hotel conference room

8

YPAR IN THE ACADEMY

It is a balmy Wednesday morning in October and we have filled the conference room in UCLA's Institute for Democracy, Education, and Access (IDEA). Colorful murals of Ella Baker, John Dewey, and youth organizers gaze upon the mass of people, laptops, and sheets of paper splayed around the conference table.

Nine of us—all at varying points in our doctoral studies—are working in some fashion with the Council. Also at the meeting is Ernest, guiding and organizing the work at hand. We have a lengthy agenda at hand to support students as they continue their summer seminar research into the school year and prepare for upcoming spring presentations. The first third of our 90-minute meeting is taken up with check-ins on the work happening at each school site, logistics for the next Saturday seminar, and other logistical information that needs to be funneled to students and teachers, such as bus tokens for transportation. We're excited about the energy that has continued to build since the end of the summer seminar. And while it is easy to get caught up in the enthusiasm about our work with the students and teachers, the bulk of today's conversation is about research, writing, and presenting. Though we are working with the students to produce an article co-authored by the entire Council, a large onus of the responsibility of disseminating and advocating for a YPAR paradigm in educational research rests with us as members of the academy.

In tracing out themes from our own field notes, observations of student learning, and analysis of our discussions with teachers, we've outlined several pathways for research articles to be developed, including analysis of youth literacies, civic education, and teacher professional development via participation in YPAR research. Ernest highlights key journals that need to hear about this work and offers framing strategies to ensure we are speaking to appropriate audiences. For some of us, these discussions will shape our dissertations and even become the first of our peer-reviewed publications. As Ernest helps us parse data sets across the research papers and we organize teams and leads for each of the papers, we are reminded of how disseminating our YPAR research is just as important a part of educational advocacy as the work we do alongside students.

Research *About* the Research *With*

For the majority of this book, we've told the story of one year within the Council of Youth Research and how the work of this cadre of teachers, students, and researchers came together. And while powerful work has been created *within* this group and disseminated through presentations, we also acknowledge that one of the key ways people have learned about our group's work is through publications *about* the group. Adult members of the Council have produced a significant body of scholarly writing about the program over the past decade, including numerous peer-reviewed journal articles written collaboratively. (See Appendix E for a list of scholarly publications written by Council members about the Council.)

As we write this, critical research and YPAR's place within the academic community is under scrutiny. As much as we would like for the Council's work to sustain ongoing methodological conversations in its own right, we are aware that the mechanisms of grant funding, peer review, and tenure and promotion within universities necessitate that adults within higher education speak *on behalf of* this work in certain venues. While we've successfully brought the entire Council to present in various academic venues, we also frequently find ourselves in these same venues describing the work on their behalf and advocating for more researchers to do the same.

In this chapter, we share some of the ways that research about YPAR work is different from other kinds of research projects, detail the institutional challenges that may be encountered, and offer suggestions for sustaining the paradigm-shifting possibilities of YPAR through single-authored and collaboratively developed writing. Though this chapter looks at YPAR from a different perspective from the one presented in the rest of the book, we feel that it is important to make transparent the ways in which YPAR work is (and is not) legitimized within the academy and outline necessary steps in the long trajectory of making YPAR a widely recognized methodology.

Building Critical Distance

Make no mistake: engaging youth in sharing findings gleaned from YPAR in presentations and publications is key to the participatory and collaborative research process. The previous chapter shared how the Council presented to peers, teachers, and nationally recognized academic communities like AERA; however, presenting and publishing *about* YPAR from the adult perspective is just as crucial. It is easy to get wrapped up in the student research cycle and spend the majority of our time supporting students, reading college applications, and keeping the program running; after all, our roots as classroom teachers make participating in this group one of the most rewarding parts of our professional lives. Being engaged in the process of learning *with* young people and mentoring powerful, critical students through high school and beyond is not only fun (and hard) work; it also contributes to our sense of purpose as critical scholars. At the same time, YPAR researchers must not lose sight of the role this research plays within the academy. This means highlighting both the research conducted *within* YPAR and empirically studying the YPAR process. These are two very different aspects that must be reconciled and discussed (usually separately).

Nevertheless, academic writing is still fundamentally aligned with the YPAR model. Sharing how the Council approaches its work, for example, represents a deliberate push for institutions of research to accept fundamentally more humanizing methodologies, as well as a push against inequitable social structures. Granted, however, the writing style and the avenues of publication are specialized, rather than inclusive. As we've illustrated throughout this book, YPAR functions as a methodological stance through revealing the ways that leveraged institutional capital *and* community wealth (Yosso, 2005) synergistically interact. As a result, we cannot disregard the fact that the goals and expectations of working within a university setting do not always neatly coalesce with the goals of community activists. To be clear, this does not mean compromising the actionable outcomes of YPAR or engaging in double-speak about the work being done. Instead, it means recognizing the *action* of YPAR from the perspective of the academy as well. We must demonstrate the validity of YPAR within proven academic measures of knowledge production and achievement. As academic researchers doing YPAR, we have an obligation to publish about this work. Our job as researchers is to produce knowledge, to change ideas, and to make new ways of thinking about and doing education possible. Why would we *not* publish about this work?

As researchers with, of, and for the Council, it was imperative for us that the work of running the Council and the work of writing about the Council got separate attention. During weekly meetings between Ernest and the graduate students, time was typically split between logistics for upcoming meetings and discussions about the various aspects of the research. Graduate students experienced these meetings as part of a deliberate model of apprenticeship into the world of academic research. We found it necessary to carefully monitor our meetings; we gave equal emphasis to the implementation of the program itself and the research being done about it. While all of us involved in the higher education side of the Council were committed to the beliefs and outcomes of this YPAR project, it was important that the Council also reflected outcomes of academic progress familiar within the educational research community. Extrapolating this more broadly, if you as a professor are creating a YPAR project and asking graduate students and colleagues to invest their time and intellectual energy into the endeavor, it should be a project that will give them valuable experience and skills that can open professional doors for them. Importantly, this does not mean simply replicating distanced models of academic service to the community; in the Council, it meant integrating graduate students into a model of academic life in which working side-by-side with community members is considered normal and necessary. The Council was not only a space in which our developing skills as researchers could be nurtured, but also a model of how to engage in critical praxis with a community as an academic.

Different and the Same

The discussion of YPAR's relevance and its place within academia is one that must be taken up and led by adult researchers. Even as young people share their work, questions remain that will always be more appropriate for adults to answer given their training and perspective. We must frame the conversation around youth in terminology that makes clear the new paradigms being forged within YPAR research today. The *value* of young people as co-researchers must be unpacked, particularly the value of honoring the voices of urban youth of color. As Duncan-Andrade (2006) explains:

> Urban youth bring unique and important insight to the dialogue about social justice. They experience the material conditions of urban poverty in visceral ways that cannot be captured through adult lenses. Sadly, schools and the larger society have failed to create avenues with which youth can discuss their understandings of the problems and conditions facing urban centers. The absence of these narratives has not only meant the increasing marginalization of urban youth, but also that insights into solutions to these problems have been overlooked.
>
> *(p. 167)*

Considering the new perspectives on youth engendered by YPAR, we want to emphasize that the purpose of academic scholarship stemming from YPAR is to help advance the academy's acceptance of valued and historically marginalized voices. Further, YPAR must guide the academy's understanding of YPAR projects as pedagogical engagements and YPAR as a challenge to positivist epistemologies and research methods. These efforts mirror what happens within YPAR projects but also differ in the specific nuances of adjusting to pre-existing frames of understanding within higher education and academic publications. It is a process of legitimation just as it is a process of community activism and social research.

What Does Our Research Look Like?

While youth were guided into familiar forms of data collection, as described in Chapters 4 and 5, researchers of YPAR within universities must be intentional about the types of data we gather, analyze, and present. The tools of academic research need to be clearly reflected and emphasized within the research *about* YPAR. This may sound obvious, but it is important to remember that the audience of the academy is often very different from the audience of community members, students, and parents. In our research about the Council we have employed a host of different qualitative methodologies, including ethnographic participant observation, case study design methodologies, focus groups, and ethnography of communication.

Describing the research in her 2010 book *Harlem on Our Minds: Place, Race, and the Literacies of Urban Youth*, Valerie Kinloch pauses near the end of her first chapter to discuss the research methods for her "participatory action research." Though her project involved fewer research participants than the Council, hewing closely to the work she conducts alongside two high school students, Phillip and Khaleeq, and their teacher, the depth of these students' lives as young men in Harlem sings across the pages. And while the sentences in the book are a deliberate mixture of Kinloch's analysis and quotes from both young men, there is a clear and deliberate *method* through which Kinloch presents her research:

> As a participant observer, I documented my observations in an ethnographic journal and participated in audio- and video-recorded sessions with youth in the community. Participants and I exchanged rhyme books or writing journals, in which we posed and openly responded to a series of self-designed questions related to schooling, community, and literacy. I formally interviewed 27 participants ranging from students to teachers and created an interview protocol for each group. However, I welcomed a diversion from format in order for participants to openly share their perspectives on a variety of topics, including writing, identity, school, gentrification, and place.
>
> *(p. 30)*

Kinloch's powerful work emphasizes the fluid nature of work *with* youth researchers and work *about* youth researchers. The above excerpt makes clear that Kinloch co-designed some research spaces alongside Phillip and Khaleeq, while she designed others on her own. For instance, the "rhyme books" mentioned above functioned as a continuing dialogue and space for brainstorming for Kinloch and the youth researchers; these could be seen as collaborative in nature. In contrast, the next sentence offers the sense that Kinloch more deliberately "formally interviewed 27 participants" (though even here she "welcomed a diversion from format" that allowed participants to guide the conversation as well). It is important, then, to recognize the flexibility that Kinloch intentionally builds into her work as a researcher. Such elasticity can be traced to traditional qualitative social science research methods *and* it provides a bedrock on which youth researchers can lay claim to their findings in venues down the road.

In a similar vein to Kinloch's work, our experiences documenting, writing about, and negotiating how we present our work within the Council echoes the adult-imposed research constraints to adhere to expectations and peer review of the academy, and also the flexibility to better align with the insights of our participants. Like Kinloch's, our work here must be able to stand alone in the contexts of single-authored publications and dissertations and also allow youth and teachers to lead advocacy work in other venues as well.

Potential and Pitfalls of YPAR in the Academy

As we write this, in 2015, YPAR is not a widely recognized form of scholarship within the academy. Within this context, we want to address some specific pragmatic concerns for scholars. We often meet colleagues, doctoral students, and teachers interested in researching YPAR. Some of the specific concerns they have addressed to us over the past decade as we've worked in this space include:

- How do you get research about YPAR published?
- Who will fund this research?
- How do you share this work on CVs and in the job-searching process?
- What challenges will you face when submitting this research to Institutional Review Boards?
- How is YPAR supported or stifled by universities?

As we address these questions, we find it important to broaden our scope beyond the Council.

Throughout this book we've deliberately hewed to the story of a single year of the Council of Youth Research. We wanted to offer the nuanced and polyphonic voices of students, teachers, graduate students, and professors engaged in the work of a YPAR project. However, as we continue this discussion of how YPAR is negotiated and understood within the academy, we also want to include the voices of several other YPAR scholars to explore various similarities and differences in how this form of research is understood, supported, and challenged in different universities.

Recently, Nicole conducted 26 interviews with professors who have coordinated prominent YPAR projects across the country. Though the key findings from this undertaking are represented elsewhere (Mirra & Rogers, forthcoming), we found that the perspectives from Nicole's interviews were fundamental to offering a wider view of YPAR within the academy. We share samples of these voices primarily because—in its nascent state as an emerging, necessary methodology— YPAR's acknowledged value varies significantly from institution to institution. Further, we want to highlight that, even as YPAR can *count* very differently for professors' tenure and promotion files, there were some strong themes that emerged across the data from these interviews regarding the status of YPAR in the academy in general. In general, we attribute quotes about YPAR to the interviewees from Nicole's research; however, when the interviewees offer frank, critical information around issues of funding and university expectations, we have anonymized these quotes. Below we attempt to delve into the specific, pragmatic concerns that emerge from *doing* YPAR as part of the academy.

Building/Leveraging University Partnerships

One aspect of YPAR that many researchers have asked us about is the process of setting up university/community partnerships. In addition to simply building a network, there is also concern about how one's department will view such partnerships. As Patrick Camangian, a professor at the University of San Francisco and co-organizer of the Step to College program notes, "Most university researchers probably discredit [YPAR] research as not being rigor[ous], and I don't think that community organizers have used rigorous research to inform their work as much as they could." Camangian's reflection points to the underlying tension that exists between the divergent purposes of the academy and organizing networks. At the root of social science projects is an emphasis on *rigorous* methodology, while organizations, schools, and other possible partners are not as immediately concerned with rigor as they are with effectiveness in organizing campaigns.

Ben Kirshner, professor at University of Colorado, Boulder and lead director of the Critical Civic Inquiry program, echoes Camangian's sentiments: "I don't think that's where universities' historical or current strengths are. We can partner with youth organizing groups but I don't think we have as much to bring to the table and it's more, I think, a research role." Kirshner later noted that there are exceptions to this statement, but in our present space within the academy he and Camangian make clear that the methods of social science research and the methods of community organizing do not mesh seamlessly. While this makes for a useful space for research and creativity—the Council has thrived in working across these boundaries—being able to translate and broker partnerships that look tenable to universities and to community organizations can be challenging.

This tension is especially apparent within the context of K–12 schools. Researchers entering these spaces can be viewed with skepticism and come up against bureaucratic walls. IRB approval, for instance, usually requires a two-step process of getting institutional approval *and* signoff from a school district. For districts that are overburdened with research requests (namely many schools located near large research institutions), the process of denying in-school research is easier than approving such requests.

In addition to successfully navigating access for community partnerships, it is important to consider what is gained, exchanged, and expected from these partnerships. For example, Jeff Duncan-Andrade, professor at San Francisco State University and founder of the Step to College program, notes that researchers should not expect equal investment and exchange as part of brokering YPAR work: "We have to bring more than we take, and we have to bring to bear the resources we bring, even if it's not the financial resources. . . There are so many resources that we can bring to districts and schools by virtue of the fact that we are university faculty." Duncan-Andrade reminds us of the service responsibility of these partnerships. How are institutions—particularly land-grant institutions— upholding the communities that they are located within? He points to a larger concern about not only fitting within traditional expectations of university part- nerships but of fundamentally altering these expectations as well.

Along these lines, Michelle Fine, professor at the City University of New York Graduate Center and advisor to the Public Science Project, also articulates a vision for altering the university partnership landscape. In her interview she said, "We're interested in the development of the researchers and of the policy and social change, but we're also interested in taking back the democratic notion of par- ticipatory science." Fine's distinction here carefully teeters between the existing academic needs of supporting researchers and the additional needs of changing the academy to be even more inclusive. Considering this statement via the lens of "pragmatic opti- mism" (Noguera, 2003), YPAR partnerships must be familiar and beneficial for academic institutions and simultaneously push toward humanizing change.

Recognizing the privileged position of working from within an institution should mean raising the knowledge base and helping enact change as part of our partnership. As Emily Ozer, a professor at University of California, Berkeley, and collaborator in a long-term partnership promoting and studying YPAR with San Francisco Peer Resources notes:

> I'm in this position as a professor where I can assist through grant writing, I can develop the evidence base that helps support the value of the work, I can do the kind of research to help identify what is working, what isn't working. I feel like there's a really valuable role, and what the [PEER program's] collaborators have told me is that, there's definitely been a kind of cache for them in terms of working with UC–Berkeley on this project. They're able to say to their funders that they're working on a UC–Berkeley collaboration.

Ozer reminds us that part of our contribution as partners is to be able to say to our collaborators that we carry with us the support and institutional capital of our home institutions. In our work with the Council, we have fre- quently heard both students and teachers at our partnering schools refer to this project as part of a large university undertaking. Though we must also strive to push for change within our universities, we should acknowledge that our institutions represent valuable capital for student resumes, for teachers to defend their practice to school administrators, and for potential grant funders to consider the work from a non-research stance (we discuss grant funding for YPAR research below as well).

Another significant factor to consider is how the university side of a YPAR partnership can act as damage control and be the face of criticality when students and teachers face push-back. For example, if students engage in critical research and unearth damning findings within a school, it is possible that presenting this data can be uncomfortable for these youth to share out. While adult researchers should be able to face occasional animosity around their findings, students are confined to existing power dynamics within schools that makes retaliation entirely too possible. As Jason Irizarry, professor at the University of Massachusetts Amherst and director of Project FUERTE, explained, students he worked with "didn't want to present to their faculty and staff for fear of retribution from the teachers, and so I spoke with the principal. I actually did some professional development with the staff, and there was tons of push-back, I mean, just insane amounts of push-back. . . The relationship, once the data started to come out, the relationship was really strained."

Key aspects of how our roles as researchers offer important contributions to schools and communities include taking the responsibility for the findings of YPAR research and ensuring that audiences that may not be receptive to this information engage with it. Ultimately, Irizarry and Fine both remind us that we must elevate YPAR above simply asking for time and resources and human capital from communities. And as Duncan-Andrade notes, we must give back in ways that create sustainable partnerships, contribute to the spaces we partner with, and take responsibility for the sometimes challenging research we encourage.

Funding

Running a group like the Council, with more than 30 students, half a dozen teachers, and another half dozen graduate students, is not something that always operates cheaply. In years that we lacked significant grant funding, the number of graduate students was scaled back significantly and group travel was limited to local events that could be reached via public transportation and carpool. On the other end of the spectrum, the Council received substantial grant funding in other years (including 2010–2011) that paid for air travel for the entire Council to AERA, for graduate student funding, and for stipends to support teachers. To be clear: while there are many resources that the Council draws upon to enact its action research, money is a driving component and one that is increasingly in short supply for critical, qualitative research today. Though it could be argued that social science research more broadly is struggling in today's climate of grant funding, the general picture of funding for YPAR may look bleak.

Funding for this research reflects how YPAR is valued within the academy. While these are often political decisions and part of a slow process of changing the culture of social science research, we must also be pragmatic about what funding looks like today and how to muster the financial resources needed in any given year. Though several researchers mentioned getting some "small grants" for their research, most researchers were also investing their own time and resources into the work of YPAR without institutional support. One interviewee aptly summarized the current state of funding of YPAR: "I haven't gotten a lot of infrastructure resources from the university for this work."

Being upfront about the intersections of graduate funding, graduate research, and investments of student time, Irizary offered a challenging anecdote:

> I had one [graduate student] funded. The first year she wasn't funded at all, she went completely as a volunteer. And then I was able to fund her the third year. Yeah, the first two years she did it without funding, and the third year I was able to fund her with a half-time graduate assistantship, and she was incredible, I mean, she was just phenomenal. The other perk was, she pulled a dissertation out of it, and so, although I couldn't compensate her as much as I would have liked to financially, you know, she was able to pull a really strong dissertation out of it, really connected with the youth, and I think, obviously, her personal and professional trajectories are transformed significantly by her interactions with the youth.

Irizary's reflection here gets to the key pragmatic challenges of YPAR. On one hand, this research approach acculturates a new generation of academics to treat YPAR as valid research and a significant model for changing the university paradigm over time. On the other hand, this same acculturation is one that indicates that volunteering one's professional time and working without the financial support of academic institutions is the norm. It is difficult to push against the systems of academic funding while also seeking financial support. Further, there is the tradeoff that critical researchers are familiar with here as well: though not receiving financial support, Irizarry's student gained significant mentorship and scholarly data and was able to produce powerful critical work as a result of her experiences with Project FUERTE.

Other researchers we talked to spoke even more directly about the frustrating nature of conducting engaged community scholarship like YPAR within academia. One interviewee noted that departments and schools of education may superficially encourage this work but not in any engrained, sustaining way: "They don't put any money into it and they don't genuinely support tenure-track faculty to do this kind of work." Though these researchers have found ways to sustain multi-year projects, they (and we) are still concerned with the sustainability of YPAR funding. Organizations have demonstrated short-term interest in one-time grants, but finding ways to sustain the costs of funding YPAR through foundations, federal grants, and university financial support has not been easy, particularly for YPAR models like the Council that depend on crucial out-of-school time for students to become apprenticed to specific communities of practice. Finding funding for the travel, teacher and graduate student stipends, materials, and food to host students on a university campus for several weeks can be difficult from one year to the next.

Further, we want to emphasize that, while financial support may be a struggle, it is worth considering the various resources available under the umbrella of research materials and supplies. From reserving rooms on campus to utilizing university libraries and harnessing colleagues' expertise, research should utilize the full extent of what is available. When considering multidisciplinary work, we have found it helpful to look for additional resources by reaching across the university to other departments (for example, seeking out GIS mapping technology). These other spaces on campus may have resources that can be made available, and such collaborations may leverage a critical mass of researchers engaged in the interests of YPAR work that can help the work gain validity within institutions down the road.

Tenure and Promotion

Just as funding represents a major struggle for individuals engaged in YPAR work in the academy, so too does the tricky process of figuring out the value of YPAR within the hiring, tenure, and promotion processes of higher education. For several researchers Nicole spoke with, much of the work of running and researching a YPAR project was counted as "service." Others were able to include this work as part of their research agendas at their universities, but this ultimately depends on the ability to publish *about* YPAR (as opposed to presenting with or publishing *with* a YPAR group). As we'll discuss in the section below, the nature of academic publishing when it comes to YPAR can feel stifling as well.

Again, we want to emphasize that YPAR work within the academy is about conducting work that can help move researchers and students further within the academy and do so with the express intention of transforming it. The critical skill sets involved in leveraging partnerships and learning within communities represent powerful, paradigm-shifting practices that new generations of academics are developing. As Duncan-Andrade noted, "We're training up a bunch of people that are going to be very powerful individual voices. And at the point when you have enough of those individual voices, then you have a movement." If we imagine YPAR work as a process of social organizing across academic institutions, we create opportunity for challenging existing notions of how we understand engaged scholarship in local communities.

Pragmatically, however, the work requirements of academic life—despite the relaxed disposition of professors portrayed in popular media—often result in our time being stretched thin. This work goes "above and beyond" the typical time commitments of teaching and research. Though it can be listed in the annual bean-counting for tenure and promotion as aspects of one's "service," we can see how the very premise of YPAR stretches across all aspects of professorial expectations; it is, by nature, an endeavor that is about teaching, research, and service. The problem is that if we assume that quality, critical, and humanizing research is an add-on to existing research requirements, we do little to address broken educational systems. Researchers like Irizarry commit extraordinary amounts of time to conducting research that is not only empirically valuable, but also crucial to bettering community relationships and training new scholars in the academy. As he noted, Project FUERTE meant "offer[ing] a course for free in an urban high school, and be[ing] there for three of the past five years. I don't get any compensation for that. I don't get any course release or anything." While this kind of time is valued for the scholarship it can eventually produce within respected peer-reviewed journals, the lack of release time here points to the need to further legitimize YPAR.

Our experience with the Council is that people like the kind of outreach that the program seems to provide from an institutional stance; however, it is too frequently not seen as research. This divide means that annual reports of academic activity need to deliberately contextualize how YPAR *is* research. When we write about YPAR we need to discuss the larger research questions we have around YPAR processes. For instance, how does YPAR offer teachers roles as powerful civic agents (Mirra & Morrell, 2011)? How does YPAR impact students' critical digital literacies (Garcia, Mirra, Morrell, Martinez, & Scorza, 2015)? What does critical democracy look like through the lens of YPAR (Mirra, Morrell, Cain, Scorza, & Ford, 2013)? In addition to the research writing done by and with the YPAR scholars, our work must point to research as it is traditionally understood by tenure and promotion committees.

Also built into the conversation of tenure and promotion is an implied need to look at the process of publishing. Ben Kirshner discusses the role of "research guilt" around YPAR publishing. As he notes, an explicit purpose of collaborative YPAR is to push toward societal and policy changes; however, that's not necessarily what peer-reviewed journals are interested in publishing. The process of explicating larger questions *around* YPAR, too, must be written about. As Kirshner said, "If you have an article that's published in a journal that really has an impact on how people think about a topic, I think that's a place where YPAR can be valuable. I don't think it should be always the goal of YPAR to do that. In fact, maybe it should only be sometimes the goal, but I do think it's a worthy goal for YPAR projects, as long as it's explicit at the beginning."

Institutional Stance

In addition to the tenure and promotion process, issues with funding, and the state of university partnerships, it is also important to recognize how YPAR intentionally addresses the institutional stances of spaces of educational research. Michelle Fine looks at the enterprise of YPAR in her work as one that is a "kind of lifting up from the history and social science radical methods and projects where social inquiry was dedicated to questions of social justice using a variety of methods, and solidarities [with] community."

Similarly, Irizarry asks of YPAR researchers, "How can we insert the heretofore silent perspective of youth [and teachers], because they're largely absent?" These central concerns voiced by Fine and Irizarry speak to how YPAR is pushing the conscience of educational research institutions. This is not simply about brokering partnerships as discussed earlier in the chapter, but about the purpose of academic research and whose voices we include in the process of research.

Scholars like Duncan-Andrade emphasize that this concern with whose knowledge is valued must be at the heart of how we do research (even as we navigate bureaucratic processes of publishing and tenure): "I don't see the point of having research skills if they're not empowering young people and creating change. I don't see the point of doing research at all if it's not meant to actually change something. And I don't see the point of working with youth if you're not intentionally aiming to engage and empower them." Building on this idea, Camangian points to the potential hypocrisy of familiar tropes of missionary models of partnership:

> It's false to believe that [diversity] projects only benefit communities of color; diversity projects also benefit the university. [They] benefit members of communities who don't have access to diverse people, and since the university benefits so much financially and socially and even ideologically and culturally from YPAR work and communities of color, it would be more equitable for them to invest in this work. And not only that; it allows them to have, to be informed by the very people they say they have an interest in learning more about serving.

Taking into account the experiences of researchers as they attempt to obtain funding, publish, and move up the academic ladder based on YPAR work, the climate around YPAR is not an easy one. As a community of researchers and academics committed to a system of education that reflects and validates humanizing, socially just research, we have a lot of work to do.

Conclusion: Continue Doing the Research

By outlining the similar tensions and challenges across YPAR programs, we want to weave together the disparate threads of what it means to be an academic researcher doing YPAR. As we have reviewed strategies and concerns around publishing, funding, and partnering with communities as part of YPAR, we also want to point to the specific ways the research of YPAR is conducted and what this says about its purpose. Emily Ozer raised a crucial question during her interview: "What's the 'value added' in terms of doing YPAR as opposed to sort of straight youth development work?" This needs to be a central question we answer in our scholarship about YPAR. If we have trouble differentiating between these two different approaches, why should our work as scholars be funded? To this point, Ozer continued:

> [YPAR and youth development] get very intertwined, particularly when young people are addressing issues that have to do with social justice and ethnic identity . . . The political piece of it is important to the youth development part and I think a lot of it depends on what they tackle, because we've now had more than 40 different projects, and there has been a huge range of [political] issues raised; I guess everything is political at school, but some things are explicitly more political than others.

YPAR is often perceived as the work of young people. As adults within the academy, it is important to consider the hours we must balance between running a project like the Council of Youth Research and conducting the research which is part of our work. Reflect on the ways that Nicole, in Chapter 6, maintained a strict to-do list and tracked the logistics of student field days. On top of that, consider the daily field notes that Ernest would write after each Council meeting. There is a corpus of work and a corpus of data that underpin the opportunities that YPAR affords youth voice. Over time, *some* aspects of this can be distributed among other members of a YPAR enterprise; however, part of the work of negotiating YPAR is done by and with adults. As critical scholars and educators, we bring YPAR into the larger academic conversation about methodologies, research stances, and funded scholarship. At this point, YPAR scholars sit at all levels of academia—we peer-review journals, evaluate conference proposals, review grant proposals, and admit new cohorts of doctoral students. We must own these positions as spaces for pushing toward the tenets of YPAR in all domains of scholarship. It is from this stance that we advocate for change; even if we are not all equipped with traditional methods of community organizing, we can help sustain new systems for societal change through YPAR.

References

Duncan-Andrade, J. (2006). Utilizing Cariño in the development of research methodologies. In J. Kincheloe, P. Anderson, K. Rose, D. Griffith, & K. Hayes (Eds.), *Urban education: An encyclopedia* (pp. 451–460). Westport, CT: Greenwood Publishing Group.

Garcia, A. (2012). *Good reception: Utilizing mobile media and games to develop critical inner-city agents of social change* (Unpublished doctoral dissertation). University of California, Los Angeles.

Garcia, A., Mirra, N., Morrell, E., Martinez, A., & Scorza, D. (2015). The Council of Youth Research: Critical literacy and civic agency in the digital age. *Reading & Writing Quarterly (31)*2, 151–167.

Kinloch, V. (2010). *Harlem on our minds: Place, race, and the literacies of urban youth.* New York: Teachers College Press.

Mirra, N., & Morrell, E. (2011). Teachers as civic agents: Toward a critical democratic theory of urban teacher development. *Journal of Teacher Education, 62*(4), 408–420.

Mirra, N., Morrell, E., Cain, E., Scorza, D., & Ford, A. (2013). Educating for a critical democracy: Civic participation re-imagined in the Council of Youth Research. *Democracy and Education 21*(1), Article 3.

Mirra, N., & Rogers, N. (in press 2015). Participation and transformation: Considering the goals and tensions of university-initiated YPAR projects with K-12 youth. *International Journal of Qualitative Studies in Education.*

Noguera, P. (2003). *City schools and the American dream: Reclaiming the promise of public education.* New York: Teachers College Press.

Yosso, T. (2005). Whose culture has capital? A Critical Race Theory of community cultural wealth. *Race, Ethnicity and Education, 8,* 69–91.

9

CONCLUSION

I look into the 40 sets of eyes around me. It is time to say something. I think about the source of words of freedom. I tell them about how I try to prepare myself for speaking powerfully. I always look for a source of motivation. Today, I tell them, we speak for all of those we have left behind to come here to this wealthy place. I ask them to look around. We are surrounded by opulence of the highest degree. The four-star hotel they're staying in is filled with ornate decorations that serve no purpose other than to remind the patrons of how fortunate they are to be surrounded by such beauty. The convention center itself is a major work of art. The shoppers walking down the streets are nicely dressed and, even during a time of economic crisis, the stores and restaurants are full. How do we not have enough money to pay for an educational system that treats students and teachers with human dignity? Why do we pretend to be poor only when it comes to educating our children, or to helping the poor? We never claim poverty during moments of international dispute.

Frederick Douglass reminds us that power concedes nothing without a demand; but power indeed concedes. Every student of history knows that change is a constant. The question is not if, but how—how we change the future. You are all change agents, I assure them. For surely you have touched everyone who has had the experience of being in your collective presence. Today will be no different. You will enter that room and change people's lives. First and foremost, you have changed each other's. You can no longer be on the sidelines. You have become actors in this drama and you have become a collective force. As for public speaking? Ninety percent of it comes from having something powerful to say; something that has to be said. As for the saying of it? I point to my mouth; some people think that the source of words is the mouth. I then point to my head; others believe that powerful words come from the mind. As I shake my head my hands rest on my belly; we know that they come from here, from the gut, from your pain and your hope and your love and your dignity and your sense of what is right and fair and true.

You speak your passion and you speak your stories. Tell them what you know to be true not just from your own stories, but from those of others you have collected in your time as critical researchers. We are here to represent these stories, we are here to let everybody know that we have work to do, but we are also here to let them know that we have cause to be hopeful. That hope is you and who you are; you members of the Council of Youth Research are the answers to all of the educational questions that matter.

We come full circle here, concluding the vignette that began in Chapter 1 as Ernest contemplated what to tell Council students about the power and meaning of their work before their AERA 2011 presentation.

Why do we need critical pedagogy? Why do we need to ponder YPAR as youth cultural production? Why do we need yet another book about theory and urban education? Because the times demand it. Because we have answers. Because we have not given up hope. Because anything is possible given enough contemplation and enough love. Perhaps our greatest fear is that we are powerful beyond measure, but we can no longer afford to be afraid. What we need is the courage to impart how critical pedagogy and cultural studies have helped us to share our stories with the world in ways that have made young people powerful beyond measure. And so we took this journey back into these discourses which, when unleashed, will demand that urban education never be the same again, dedicating our work to the Council of Youth Research and to all of those who have been inspired by them and their example.

In today's public educational landscape (at least in the United States), the lifespan of students' compulsory public education is—for most—13 years long. For a large portion of U.S. working poor and youth of color, this length is statistically much less. Our ability to positively impact the world of elementary and secondary education and to posit change with and for young people hinges on borrowed time. While it can be easy to see a year within the Council as one of many cycles of research and growth in our professional careers, we must remember that it constitutes a significant time commitment from students in a relatively short schooling career.

While YPAR is pushing toward powerful shifts in the paradigms of social science research methodology, the glacial pace at which we can patiently wait for progress within the academy is untenable for the students and teachers who toil in the "trenches" of public education. At the end of the year, recognizing that a handful of students will head to college and a new cadre of students will join the CYR family, what kind of *value* can we say we've provided? It's a question that YPAR projects at large must confront. Sure, the work may look flashy. Students may get fired up about issues of justice. Researchers may get a handful of accolades to sprinkle across lengthy CVs. But what is the benefit to the communities that we must hold ourselves responsible to? How—substantively— are participants within a YPAR project, as well as the community that such a project emerges from, better than they were 365 days ago? Spinning this out further, let's say a YPAR project is funded on a three-year cycle that echoes common foundation timelines: consider the time invested by students and teachers during this length of time. How much do we value the members of our YPAR communities? Can we ensure we have made our research morally worthy of the co-researchers we draw in?

We've been able to articulate a clear narrative about youth and learning from our work in the Council over the past 15 years. That is: if you create spaces where young people are able to work authentically on projects that have real meaning to them, if you create modes of participation where they get to become something as they're learning something, where their learning is connected to identity, these spaces become powerful spaces for re-making students' academic and intellectual trajectories. One of the key goals we seek to achieve is to help young people see themselves navigating institutions like colleges and local government offices and helping them to leverage their love for their communities and their language and literacy practices outside of school settings into the ability to navigate formal institutions of school. If we discontinued our attempts to address these problems, the Council would be far less attractive to us as a pedagogical revolution.

As we write this, there exists a decade and a half's worth of students, teachers, and researchers who have committed to research and advocacy related to school equity in Los Angeles. Our Council of Youth Research is a family with roots spread throughout the infrastructure of Los Angeles. Each new member is strengthened by those who came before, and we stress to students their responsibility to uphold the rigor of the Council for those who follow in their footsteps. Indeed, tradition and apprenticeship is important for YPAR endeavors and becomes transparently so when this work is seen as something that does not end with a single report. The cycles of YPAR grow in concentric circles that challenge hegemony and amplify the voices and actions of students and teachers.

Sustaining a Movement

Just as YPAR expands the audience to whom we must hold our research accountable, so too does it place the onus of sustainability on more than just our shoulders, as members of the academy. Instead, if we build from the premise that we research *for* and research *with* the young people as we strive together for social equity, we must demand support for this work from across society as well. In previous chapters, we have highlighted ways that community members, local organizations, and government officials were drawn into the work of the Council. Each relationship forged represents another opportunity to build critical allies for educational equity.

Large-scale funding is not going to fall into the laps of YPAR researchers anytime soon. This is particularly true if the focus of some YPAR projects is to challenge critiques of capitalist and hegemonic practices that underlie some of the biggest names in educational philanthropy. Considering this context, what does compensation for our time *mean*? If we see significant changes in educational pathways over time, better academic outcomes from the students we work with, and support for students to take up this work on their own, perhaps that is a return on our invested time and energies.

A critique that the Council has received is that it is expensive. We're told that for the amount of money it costs to operate this project, thousands more students than the handful we work with each year could be impacted through smaller-scale interventions. And yet, considering the stories we have shared about how this work has transformed young people's lives, would anyone begrudge the dollars spent? We aimed to show what is possible within YPAR projects when they are well-funded to allow us to imagine the kinds of learning opportunities to which every student is entitled and encourage innovation.

As we write this, public education systems are vastly undercompensating the time of teachers and professors across the country. Our professions are stratified by discussions of tenure, seniority, funding, and student performance. For those of us privileged to take up precious seats within universities or to have opportunities to work with young people in our classrooms on a daily basis, we know that our time is never fully compensated in terms of total hours we may put into "work." And while this fact is not acceptable and must change, it also does not give us an excuse for not taking up YPAR as career-long actions. Considering the implications of YPAR for changing the educational landscape in the 21st century, we need to find sustainability that exists beyond the overly competitive sources of funding.

When we think of "sustaining" we also think, reflexively, of "sustenance." We are reminded of Antonio, Ebony, and Mark's discussion in the interlude about brokering relationships about the need to feed ourselves and our Council family in a literal way. Sustaining is about feeling alive, maintaining energy, and loving oneself enough to persevere with the work we must do. To this extent, how does the YPAR work that you are undertaking get you out of bed excited for work? How does it keep you up at night in anticipation? If the "work" of YPAR isn't sustaining you intellectually, emotionally, or professionally, it is time to rethink the foundations of the work. What kind of community have you developed and how can this community become one that is supportive and resilient?

What is YPAR Worth?

How do we measure the *value* of YPAR over time? Within the Council we can count the number of peer-reviewed articles that have been pushed forward around research agendas that include the Council's momentum. We can count the grant dollars that have (occasionally) supported this work. We can count the partnerships that this work has fostered with the schools, teachers, and administration that have worked closely with the Council and with a bevy of nonprofits and city offices that have hosted Council events and assisted with data collection. But most of all, we can look to the students. They speak volumes for the work of YPAR at large and the Council of Youth Research in particular. To date, almost every student that has participated in the Council has gone on to college.

Within the world of academic intervention and educational reform, there are easier narratives and there are tougher narratives. One of the easier narratives to tell about the Council is that it represents a higher quality of literacy instruction than what students in the schools we are working with are typically receiving. There has been no real push-back on this as a unique and innovative pedagogic space that is exciting young people. The academic value of the Council stands as a strong narrative. This is a space for developing academic literacies, digital literacies, connections to the humanities, writing, social studies, and civic literacies. These are things we've measured empirically over the life of the Council. We know this is part of the value of YPAR within educational settings.

On the other hand, it has been harder, epistemologically, to say that having young people do research in this way is an important way to think about research. The funding has never come from that. No one has ever funded the Council to do critical research; it has always been about teacher learning or student learning or college trajectories. As a result, we must start thinking about YPAR as an epistemological struggle. We are, only now, at the very beginning of this struggle.

And in recognizing this work as a struggle, we are reminded—again and again—that this work is morally important. Going back to our initial claims in the introduction of this book, if we really do believe in the full humanity of young people, that their voices are valid and should be heard in spaces that make decisions about their schooling experiences, then YPAR is not an extracurricular endeavor but an imperative mandate. We *must* further this work and be active in the pedagogical struggle to bring youth voices and insights into the field of educational research. As the adults spearheading much of this work, we must remember the ways the four letters of YPAR intersect deliberately. Thinking about ours as work focused on youth, and participation, and action, and research, we must consider how we are holding up young people as having legitimate voices in both teaching and research spaces.

We are on the precipice of a new research and educational paradigm. We must remember that this is about fostering humanity within spaces of research for both youth and adults. In doing so, the acts of learning, asking questions, and advocating together become humanizing for all involved and transform into acts of revolutionary love.

APPENDIX A

In Their Own Words: Students Explain the Council of Youth Research

Raising Our Voices: Young, Critical Minds Influencing Education Policy
By the Council of Youth Research (Fall 2011)

The Council of Youth Research is a Los Angeles–based group of passionate youth and adults engaged in Youth Participatory Action Research. The group consists of African-American and Latino high school students from high schools throughout Los Angeles. Along with teachers and university graduate students, we research issues that our schools and communities face. We students have at least one thing in common: our families want us to have better academic lives than what they experienced. We are trying to fulfill their hopes. We don't come from areas where we're surrounded by success. In fact, many of us go to schools where the graduation rates aren't very high. For example, at Manual Arts High School, one of the schools in the Council of Youth Research, the graduation rate is about 48%. More than half of the students are not graduating from high school. The Council of Youth Research is here to figure out why this is happening and how we can fix these issues we face at school. We're a group of ordinary high school students who care about the way we experience high school.

The Council of Youth Research is made up of groups of students—mostly juniors and seniors—from five high schools: Manual Arts, Locke, Crenshaw, Wilson, and Roosevelt. Our schools reflect the demographics of the surrounding communities of South and East Los Angeles. We see these areas as one big community. We are all the same people—different races, but the same people. Crenshaw High School is located in a traditionally African-American community in South Los Angeles that has changed recently as Latino families have moved into the area. Now, the school serves 65% African-American students and 33% Latino students. Locke High School, also in South Los Angeles, is also located in a neighborhood that has seen recent demographic change. About 67% of the students at Locke are Latino and 31% are African-American. Manual Arts High School, at the northern part of South Los Angeles, is 81% Latino and 19% African-American. Roosevelt High School and Wilson High School, both in East Los Angeles, are 99% and 93% Latino, respectively. All of our communities have been hubs of activism in recent history, starting in the 1960s.

Reflecting trends in Los Angeles and the nation, three of the five high schools are run completely or partially by nonprofit organizations outside of district control. Locke High School is run by the charter organization Green Dot; Roosevelt High School is run by the Partnership for Los Angeles Schools (also called "the mayor's partnership"), and Manual Arts High School is run partially by L.A.'s Promise. Crenshaw High School and Wilson High School, on the other hand, are run by the Los Angeles Unified School District.

All of our schools—whether run by charter organizations or by the school district—are public schools and lack resources compared to wealthier schools. This means that the schools haven't made enough investment in the education of us students. We don't get what we really need in order to succeed. Our schools lack money for books, teachers, and supplies.

In the Council of Youth Research, we take on problems in our community in order for our community members and peers to benefit. The Council has taken on problems such as lack of access to healthy food, lack of space for students to express themselves, unequal distribution of technology, being unable to use technology in the classroom, and inequitable access to quality curriculum.

By analyzing the problems in our community, we attempt to find ways to solve them. When we were faced with a lack of access to healthy food, we came up with the solution of a garden. When we were faced with a lack of space for students to express themselves, we came up with the solution of a teen support group. When it came to not being able to use technology in the classroom, we tried to incorporate Facebook into everyday classes. When it came to access to quality curriculum, we came up with a student-led professional development workshop for teachers. In this way, we hope to continue to find solutions to the problems we have to face in our community and turn defects into assets.

Another one of our responsibilities is taking part in trips, conferences, and meetings. In past years we have presented at American Educational Research Association conferences and at events for community members and educational stakeholders. At these conferences and events, we strengthen our sense of being a family. On our most recent conference trip, some new Council members were surprised by the amount of love there was among students who don't even go to the same high schools. Maybe what brings us together is the idea that we can change how students in the future are educated.

We keep this idea in mind as we make our presentations, remembering that we have to speak for the students and community members who aren't on stage with us. If outsiders don't hear what we have to say, then all that will be left for them to hear will be the negative things said about our schools and communities. This is why it is important for all our voices to be heard.

The Summer Seminar and School-Year Component

There are two components of the Council: the summer seminar and the school-year component. The summer seminar lasts several weeks in July and/or August and is held on the campus of the University of California, Los Angeles. The school-year component involves meetings at the individual school sites and whole-group meetings at UCLA.

During our most recent summer seminar, we arrived at 9 in the morning and left at 5 in the afternoon (or later!). We started the morning with workshops led by the graduate student researchers from UCLA. These workshops were based on education theory from Paulo Freire, Angela Valenzuela, Daniel Solorzano, and Tara Yosso. We learned about pedagogy, hegemony, and what it means to be Students of Color in an unjust system. We were thrilled and proud to be high school students exposed to graduate-level readings from educational theorists. Little did we know that these methods would ultimately help us narrow down topics for our research projects.

At every summer seminar, there are youth who leave to go to college and new members are introduced in the Council. At the most recent seminar, the new additions were unfamiliar with everyone and did not know any other student that was not from their particular schools. For all youth, there was some uncertainty within ourselves as we were challenged to work among one another. The first few days were the hardest. You could feel the awkwardness; we were all very timid, and we were quiet because we felt that we lacked knowledge about certain subjects and our opinions were not good enough.

As the days progressed, however, we were able to get acquainted with one another, as we were placed into not only school-based groups, but also mixed groups consisting of students from each of the five schools. Our assignment as a mixed group was to break down and explain one of five key components toward conducting a proper research project: choosing research topics, collecting and analyzing data, creating video documentaries, and advocating for our communities. Additionally, our summer seminar expanded our knowledge of current-day issues, such as the school-to-prison pipeline, budget cuts, and other issues that impacted us, which we learned about through daily lectures. From our summer seminar, we were able to incorporate all of this information to explain and analyze the dilemmas we faced as Students of Color attending low-income schools.

Through the summer seminar, we were able to relate educational research to our own individual lives; thus, we felt our research questions were really based on the oppressive conditions that affected us as students on a daily basis. We began to analyze what we deemed "normal" and were able to understand that our educational system is not fair for all students, for we as Students of Color were not given the essential materials, such as up-to-date technology, new books, or essential class materials. It was this awakening that began the journey toward our research topics for our school-based groups.

We realized that we were about to transform the system by learning about it, analyzing it, and finding ways to fix these problems in order to attain educational justice. We would not only be speaking from our own personal experience but from the data and statistics we gained through our research. Once we were able to understand the process to conduct such research, we were able to begin thinking about possible research questions, which we would finalize during the school year. In this way, the activities of the summer seminar ensured that we had a structured and productive school year.

Throughout the school year, we spend most of our time in our school-based groups, which include four or more students, a teacher, and a university graduate student advisor. Each of these five groups meets once a week after school in preparation for our conferences. The early stages of our projects are crucial. Here, students from each school, respectively, share their ideas to settle on research questions that we would like to focus on. Our central questions are achieved through a series of revisions and discussions. Not only do the students in our group play a role in deciding our research questions, but our teacher and graduate school advisor also help make decisions. In addition, some of our school-based groups partner with community organizations, which also provide input about the questions. Once we've clarified our research questions, we begin to research the issue, using quantitative and qualitative research tools such as surveys and interviews as a means to prove or disprove our research claim. After distributing and collecting numerous surveys, along with conducting several interviews, our weekly meetings gradually turn into almost daily meetings. We compile, analyze, and organize all of our data into a PowerPoint presentation to be presented to educators all across the nation. The process is long, but rewarding.

In addition to these meetings, we meet as a whole group every month at UCLA, where we update each other and discuss our unique research projects. Meeting with the rest of the team at UCLA is truly invaluable and enriching. We all receive guidance on our projects and are given the opportunity to communicate with students and teachers from other schools in the area. This allows us to form connections with others and voice our individual experiences. Seeing how passionate the school groups are about their research topics reinforces everyone's passion and intensifies our desire for change. The primary purpose of our project is both to expose the issues within our schools and communities and to propose positive solutions to these problems. We are unfolding the truth. We are calling for change.

Studying Policymakers

During both the summer seminar and the school year, we communicate with policymakers and study them. From conducting research with the Council of Youth Research, we realize that policymakers greatly affect the community and people. For example, the legislation stemming from the *Williams v. California* case, a class-action lawsuit, affected education statewide because it tried to ensure that every student had access to high-quality education. Studying policymakers helps us further understand how we can influence them to create policies that bring equitable education to all students in America. In doing this research, we realized that there are many different aspects that go into play when policymakers create policies, and it's our jobs to determine why that is and to pinpoint what all those varying aspects are.

We interview policymakers because we want to hear their thoughts and responses about youth like us not receiving the quality of education we deserve. In the summer of 2010, the Council of Youth Research traveled to Sacramento to interview policymakers about how we are not provided quality education in our schools. As we asked them hard-hitting questions on specific topics, they were astounded by us, but they sometimes did not take us seriously. They tried to answer with simple and vague responses and they eventually even avoided answering questions by asking us questions. For instance, Kevin Johnson, the mayor of Sacramento, disregarded what we were talking about and tried to keep us off topic. He tried to bribe us and distract us with money for answering questions that had nothing to do with why we were there.

Through these experiences, we learned that policymakers have manipulative ways to make people feel like they have no power. Politicians view us youth as "subjects," not really knowing that the choices they make can affect our lives and futures in an enormous way. When we talk to policymakers, we believe that they learn that youth aren't careless or dismissive. Policymakers realize that we don't have the mentality that they think we have. They learn that we do actually care about the policies that are being made, which affect our daily lives. When we talk to policymakers, they learn that we take everything seriously and we want change in the educational system.

Through our research, we realized that challenging policymakers and asking questions about policies that affect us really puts policymakers on the defensive. Questions like, "Who did you intentionally create these policies for?" and "Why do certain policies that you create affect people differently?" really make policymakers feel uncomfortable. We realized that it's important to keep asking questions that matter to us and to keep finding the answers that ultimately impact us. After persistently trying, we found that the truth usually has a way of getting out. We are able to find the root causes of the problems in education and why these policymakers really created some of these policies.

Sharing Our Research within Our Schools and Communities

The research we do has a great deal of impact on our interactions with peers, teachers, and our communities. Through our research we are able to affect people's ways of thinking and what they do. Researching and showcasing our research changes how we relate to our peers because we want to share what we have learned with them to make them more knowledgeable. We also strive to get them to become critical thinkers and to get them involved so they will help bring about the change we are moving toward.

The relationship with our educators changes also because we are no longer just students; we are creators of knowledge. We move from being receivers to givers, not just to our peers but also to our own educators. We serve as a bridge between them and the rest of the student body. We become equals in some aspects because we are both moving toward the betterment of our communities. The relationship between us and the community also undergoes a drastic change because our research reaches out to the severely uninformed and pulls them into an atmosphere of progress and change which motivates them to become agents of the change. Through our research we give ourselves the tools to be able to hold our own against waves of opposition, and motivate people to rise up and stand next to us against all the injustices we face.

The way the Wilson High School group communicates its research to others is by doing presentations at different events. We communicate to students, parents, and community members to inform them about the issues that affect the school and community and to get them involved.

This group helped an organization called the Asian Pacific American Legal Center in creating a garden for the community. Part of the work involved encouraging the community to participate in growing their own gardens and staying active. In order to disseminate information, there are meetings at Wilson that are open for everyone in the school and community.

The Locke High School group spread its message by organizing workshops and presenting at conferences for teachers. They support an organization called the Association of Raza Educators by helping to organize events and participation in the events. They educate the community to help them fight for equal education rights.

Like Locke, the Roosevelt High School group shares information by doing presentations and helping an organization called Inner City Struggle reach out to the community through events such as workshops. Roosevelt's work with this organization led to the end of truancy tickets for students as they helped mobilize the community into action.

The Manual Arts High School group has given presentations to teachers at the school. For instance, in 2010, the group led a professional development workshop for teachers about how to enact high-quality curriculum in their classrooms.

The Crenshaw High School group members present to their own classes as well as at events. For example, they gave a presentation at California State University, Dominguez Hills. They have had a strong impact on teachers and members of the community by presenting about their use of technology in schools. The group works with the Coalition for Education Justice, an activist group where they meet to talk about issues and find solutions to make the community better. They protest for everyone to live a better life. Everyone has a voice, so make sure yours is heard!

Sharing Our Research with Broader Audiences

In addition to sharing our research within our schools and communities, we disseminate our research to broader audiences through presentations at conferences and events, our blog, and a website. In years past, the culminating task for our summer seminar was to present our research that we conducted with the guidance of teachers and graduate students at Los Angeles City Hall. We had the opportunity to share and discuss our findings, and more importantly, to share the demands we have to improve the quality of public education for students in the communities of South Central and East Los Angeles. At these presentations we were able to inform city officials of the educational issues that their constituencies faced.

We also moved beyond our city limits to share our work on a state level too. As we described earlier in the chapter, in the summer of 2010, we traveled to the capital city of Sacramento, California, to conduct interviews with various elected officials, such as former Superintendent of Public Instruction Jack O'Connell, current Mayor of Sacramento Kevin Johnson, and the former Speaker of the California State Assembly and now Congressmember Karen Bass. We took these opportunities to discuss the current findings of our research and developed our interview questions accordingly. We understood that we are the direct representatives and link between our communities and institutional power and saw ourselves as consultants in addition to interviewers.

Not only did we have opportunities to share our work directly with elected officials, but we also have consistent opportunities to share our work on a national and even international level. The American Educational Research Association (AERA) is an organization that holds an annual conference attracting thousands of educational professionals from around the world to discuss current work in education. We participated in sharing our research at this conference in 2009, 2010, and 2011. The Council of Youth Research has set a precedent of incorporating the presence of youth at these conferences, not as attendees, but as educational researchers. Our work presence at this conference serves as affirmation that high school students have the capacity to conduct graduate-level research and have direct insight into the impacts of educational policy.

Our work continues to be shared continually and is easily accessible through a website and our blog. We are featured under the projects category of UCLA's Institute of Democracy, Education & Access's website: www.idea.gseis.ucla.edu. You can find an archive of our past work, most notably the PowerPoint presentations and short documentaries we have used at the websites for the Los Angeles City Hall, AERA, our respective schools, and community events. Our blog, at youngcriticalminds.com, chronicles our individual experiences as youth researchers and the impact our work has had on us individually and as a collective. Our aim with these websites is to share our work with others and show how work is conducted. All this work we do is not easy; we spend many hours during the summer learning, many more hours after school and even on weekends analyzing educational and social theory, developing our data collection methods, analyzing qualitative and quantitative data, and creating powerful and accessible presentations and media. We document this humanizing process through our blog.

Conclusion

Confident, driven, and empowered—this is what we feel being in the Council. Before we joined the Council, we didn't realize the potential we have as youth. We had different mentalities. In general, people underestimate us, view us as incompetent, and have low expectations of us. But if we are given the right tools and support, we can break down these stereotypes and make an impact. For example, in the Council we are given the tools to collect and analyze data, including cameras, surveys, and theories. We also learn how to put them to use and learn interviewing skills. As a collective group we come together and formulate our own conclusions and present our findings to national audiences and national organizations like AERA.

In the Council, we are more than just researchers; we are also advocates and representatives of the youth in our schools. Unfortunately, not many youth in urban schools advocate, let alone know the issues that they face in their schools. In the Council we become aware of our surroundings and the issues that affect our education. For example, during one summer seminar, we went to Beverly Hills High School. When we made comparisons with the urban schools we attend, we found that our schools pale in comparison. We found that education in public schools isn't equal as it should be according to the case settlement in *Williams v. California.*

Not only did we become aware through the Council—we spread that awareness as well. We've impacted teachers, graduate students, and educators across the spectrum in changing their curricula and the ways they view youth in education. After our presentations, people see us as capable and feel inspired to incorporate the work we do with their students or others. We break traditions by virtue of us, as youth, presenting our research to national audiences, like that of the AERA conference. Knowing that we impact others as youth, we feel inspired and find passion in our work to keep going. We feel extremely capable and competent to do graduate-level research. We plan to continue influencing educators and policymakers through our work, and we hope to inspire other youth to realize the power of their voices.

APPENDIX B

2010 Summer Seminar Reading List

I. Critical Social Theory

Fine, M., Bloom, J., & Chajet, L. (2003). Betrayal: Accountability from the bottom. Special issue on *Rethinking Accountability, VUE 1*, 8–19.

Freire, P. (1970). Chapter 2. In *Pedagogy of the oppressed* (pp. 71–82). New York: Continuum.

Ladson-Billings, G. (2006). From the achievement gap to the education debt: Understanding achievement in U.S. schools. *Educational Researcher, 35*(7), 3–12.

Ladson-Billings, G., & Tate, W. (1995). Toward a critical race theory of education. *Teachers College Record, 97*(1), 47–68.

MacLeod, J. (1987). Social reproduction in theoretical perspective. In *Ain't no makin' it: Aspirations and attainment in a low-income neighborhood* (pp. 11–24). Boulder: Westview.

Valenzuela, A. (1999). Excerpt from *Subtractive schooling: U.S.-Mexican youth and the politics of caring*. Ithaca: State University of New York Press.

Yosso, T. (2005). Whose culture has capital? A critical race theory discussion of community cultural wealth. *Race, Ethnicity and Education, 8*(1), 69–91.

II. Education in the Courts (*Williams v. California* and *Robles-Wong v. California*)

Fine, M., Burns, A., Payne, Y., & Torre, M. (2004). Civics lessons: The color and class of betrayal. *Teachers College Record, 106*(11), 2193–2223.

Oakes, J. (2004). Investigating the claims in Williams v. State of California: An unconstitutional denial of education's basic tools. *Teachers College Record, 106*(11), 1889–1906.

Summary of *Robles-Wong v. California* (2010)

Williams v. California Complaint (2000)

Williams v. California Settlement Overview (2005)

APPENDIX C

UCLA/IDEA Council of Youth Research Survey: The State of Education in California

1. Please choose the response that reflects your opinion about each of the following statements.

	Strongly Disagree	Disagree	Agree	Strongly Agree	Rating Average	Response Count
The state is providing me with an adequate education.	5.4% (34)	15.4% (96)	**67.0% (419)**	12.2% (76)	2.86	625
The state is providing me with a powerful, internationally competitive education.	7.2% (45)	33.6% (210)	**50.9% (318)**	8.3% (52)	2.60	625
The state is spending enough money on public schools.	31.7% (198)	**47.7% (298)**	17.0% (106)	3.7% (23)	1.93	625
The state government is meeting my educational needs.	10.4% (65)	38.4% (240)	**47.2% (295)**	4.0% (25)	2.45	625
				answered question		625
				skipped question		0

2. Please choose the response that reflects your opinion about each of the following statements.

	Strongly Disagree	Disagree	Agree	Strongly Agree	Rating Average	Response Count
My teachers care about me and prepare me for the future.	4.5% (28)	11.1% (69)	**59.8% (373)**	24.7% (154)	3.05	625
My teachers are often observed by administration.	7.5% (47)	33.0% (206)	**51.3% (320)**	8.2% (51)	2.60	624
My teachers communicate well with my parents.	14.7% (92)	36.7% (229)	**39.9% (249)**	8.7% (54)	2.42	624
My teachers value my culture and ideas through their teaching.	8.8% (55)	30.1% (188)	**49.7% (310)**	11.4% (71)	2.64	624
My teachers are excellent.	8.2% (51)	27.7% (173)	**48.1% (300)**	16.0% (100)	2.72	624
				answered question		624
				skipped question		1

3. Please choose the response that reflects your opinion about each of the following statements.

	Strongly Disagree	Disagree	Agree	Strongly Agree	Rating Average	Response Count
The curriculum in my classes is preparing me for a job.	10.6% (66)	34.3% (214)	**43.1% (269)**	12.0% (75)	2.57	624
The curriculum in my classes is preparing me for college.	4.3% (27)	16.7% (104)	**57.5% (359)**	21.5% (134)	2.96	624
The curriculum in my classes is challenging.	4.5% (28)	29.0% (181)	**53.8% (336)**	12.7% (79)	2.75	624
Students are involved in creating curriculum at this school.	11.1% (69)	34.8% (217)	**47.4% (296)**	6.7% (42)	2.50	624
The curriculum in my classes relates to me and the real world.	9.6% (60)	35.6% (222)	**47.4% (296)**	7.4% (46)	2.53	624
				answered question		624
				skipped question		1

4. Please choose the response that reflects your opinion about each of the following statements.

	Strongly Disagree	Disagree	Agree	Strongly Agree	Rating Average	Response Count
My school offers special academic programs and after-school activities.	4.4% (27)	11.0% (68)	**54.4% (337)**	30.3% (188)	3.11	620
There are enough social services available in my community.	7.9% (49)	35.2% (218)	**48.9% (303)**	8.1% (50)	2.57	620
My school has enough technology available to students.	17.6% (109)	**41.9% (260)**	34.4% (213)	6.1% (38)	2.29	620
I have a class and home set of textbooks that are up to date and in good condition.	15.0% (93)	32.7% (203)	**42.4% (263)**	9.8% (61)	2.47	620
My school has enough learning materials (ex. paper).	11.1% (69)	32.7% (203)	**44.7% (277)**	11.5% (71)	2.56	620
				answered question		620
				skipped question		5

5. Please choose the response that reflects your opinion about each of the following statements.

	Strongly Disagree	Disagree	Agree	Strongly Agree	Rating Average	Response Count
The adults at my school REALLY care about me.	12.6% (78)	32.4% (200)	**46.9% (290)**	8.1% (50)	2.50	618
The restrooms at my school are clean and open to students.	29.4% (182)	**40.5% (250)**	25.4% (157)	4.7% (29)	2.05	618
I don't eat at school often because I dislike the taste of the food.	15.9% (98)	**29.1% (180)**	27.7% (171)	27.3% (169)	2.67	618
My school serves healthy food.	16.8% (104)	**40.0% (247)**	38.7% (239)	4.5% (28)	2.31	618
My school should have more green space (ex. grass, plants, trees).	5.2% (32)	23.8% (147)	**43.7% (270)**	27.3% (169)	2.93	618
My school looks and feels like a prison (ex. bars, gates, food)	13.6% (84)	**33.3% (206)**	30.4% (188)	22.7% (140)	2.62	618
				answered question		618
				skipped question		7

6. Please choose the response that reflects your opinion about each of the following statements.

	Strongly Disagree	Disagree	Agree	Strongly Agree	Rating Average	Response Count
My principal is doing a good job.	11.2% (69)	24.0% (148)	**53.8% (332)**	11.0% (68)	2.65	617
My principal works with parents and students in making school decisions.	12.6% (78)	36.1% (223)	**44.7% (276)**	6.5% (40)	2.45	617
District administrators are meeting my educational needs.	8.8% (54)	37.4% (231)	**49.4% (305)**	4.4% (27)	2.49	617
My voice is taken into consideration at my school.	19.8% (122)	**42.0% (259)**	34.4% (212)	3.9% (24)	2.22	617
Students at my school are prepared to step up and become leaders.	12.0% (74)	32.9% (203)	**44.2% (273)**	10.9% (67)	2.54	617
				answered question		**617**
				skipped question		**8**

7. I consider my educational leaders to be (choose all that apply):

	Response Percent	Response Count
Teachers	**68.6%**	**423**
Students	35.7%	220
Parents	46.5%	287
Administration	20.7%	128
Government	7.5%	46
	answered question	**617**
	skipped question	**8**

8. What school do you attend?

	Response Count
	613
answered question	**613**
skipped question	**12**

9. What is your home zip code?

	Response Count
	613
answered question	**613**
skipped question	**12**

10. What is your gender?

	Response Percent	Response Count
Female	44.0%	270
Male	**56.0%**	**343**
answered question		**613**
skipped question		**12**

11. What is your race/ethnicity? (Choose all that apply)

	Response Percent	Response Count
Latino/Hispanic	**70.0%**	**429**
African-American	26.8%	164
Asian	6.9%	42
Native-American	4.4%	27
White	4.2%	26
answered question		**613**
skipped question		**12**

12. What grade will you enter in the fall?

	Response Percent	Response Count
9th	13.5%	83
10th	18.1%	111
11th	29.7%	182
12th	**38.7%**	**237**
answered question		**613**
skipped question		**12**

APPENDIX D

YPAR Symposium Proposal Submitted to the 2011 Annual Meeting of the American Educational Research Association

Session Title

Blending Youth Participatory Action Research and Youth Organizing: Analyzing the Council of Youth Research

Abstract

This session explores the Council of Youth Research as a community of practice that positions urban youth as powerful civic agents through engaging them in youth participatory action research (YPAR) and transformative community action. This session will highlight the voices of high school student researchers, who will discuss their research with youth and community organizing groups and analyze the dialectic relationship between research and organizing. The students, teachers, and university researchers involved in the program will explain the theoretical and practical impacts that their work has on new media pedagogy, civic engagement, and literacy learning. We will present this work as the starting point for a multi-site and multi-modal movement for educational justice led by young people.

Session Summary

The Council of Youth Research is a community of high school students, teachers, university professors, and graduate student researchers committed to conducting research aimed at improving conditions in urban schools and injecting the voices of young people into conversations around education policy and reform. The students and teachers in the program hail from high schools in East Los

Angeles, South Central Los Angeles, and Watts—all communities within Los Angeles that suffer disproportionately from concentrated poverty, systemic racism, and under-performing schools but also draw strength from deep historical traditions of organizing and resistance.

This session will analyze how the Council translates the theory of youth participatory action research (YPAR) into practice and engages with community organizations to enact transformative change. The questions we explore include:

1. How does participation in the Council facilitate identity development in the areas of citizenship, literacy, and digital media participation? What supports and pedagogical practices enable this development?
2. How are the young people in the Council of Youth Research attempting to forge a new relationship between YPAR and youth organizing?

Each paper in this session will highlight a different facet of the Council's work. The first paper will examine how the practices of YPAR and community organizing foster student agency and empowerment. The second paper will analyze how the Council utilizes participatory digital media tools to expand the scope and power of research and action efforts. The third paper explains how the Council is redefining civic engagement for urban youth and contributing to a more participatory vision of democratic life. The fourth paper analyzes how the Council operates as a community of practice in which learning intersects with identity development through critical literacy practices. Each paper will privilege student and teacher presenters.

All of the papers will seek to examine the extent to which the Council of Youth Research draws upon a foundation of education for democracy and transformation (Dewey 1932; Freire 1970), learning through cultural modeling (Lee, 2007), intense community participation (Lave & Wenger, 1991; Rogoff, 2003), community and youth organizing (Ginwright & James, 2002; Mediratta, Shah, & McAlister, 2009), and collaborative participatory action research (Cammarota & Fine, 2008; McIntyre, 2000; Morrell, 2004).

This session will provide audience members with an in-depth case study of the successes and challenges involved in fostering a space in which young people can develop a research agenda, conduct research, and present their work to stakeholders. Through the use of critical epistemologies and intensive case-study methodologies involving testimonials, critical discourse analysis, ethnographic observation, and counter-storytelling, each paper will provide crucial insight into the many elements at play in communities of practice oriented toward action.

This interactive session will privilege the voices of young people and actively involve the audience in collaborative dialogue about YPAR and its dialectical relationship with community and youth organizing. We hope that this session encourages the educational research establishment and classroom educators to connect research to school and community action led by youth.

Individual Papers

Challenging Notions of "Legitimate" Research and Teaching: Council of Youth Researchers Embodying a Critical Pedagogy

In this paper, the students, teachers, and university researchers of the Council of Youth Research challenge the discourse of traditional education research and reform and shift attention to the ways that young people develop critical consciousness and build expertise as critical pedagogues through action research and organizing efforts. To best understand the ways in which youth researchers take up the positions of critical pedagogues, we utilize a critical qualitative approach which analyzes video footage of student presentations, examines artifacts from our participatory action research projects (e.g., documentaries, student videos, PowerPoint presentations, written pieces, and reflections), and reviews extensive field notes.

Navigating a world that negates the lives of Black and Brown communities can be a daunting task for youth of color. Some students are aware of the ways in which the experience of schooling pushes them from a positive sense of cultural and linguistic identity toward an active denial of self in order to navigate a system of domination under which white, middle-class values set the standards for success (Valenzuela, 1999). Because of this, there is a need for more engaging pedagogies that draw from the experiences of youth to create new forms of knowledge. This pedagogical approach is essential because it values the voices of youth from marginalized communities which offer further understanding of the structural and cultural failure of urban education (Duncan-Andrade & Morrell, 2008).

We seldom think about the ways in which youth enact critical pedagogy in their resistance against oppressive conditions. Oftentimes, the literature surrounding critical pedagogy highlights the roles adults play in facilitating the learning process of young people. In this paper, we look at the critical pedagogy that urban youth develop as they engage in youth participatory action research in and around their schools and communities.

Specifically, we analyze the powerful, nuanced ways that the Council students present research findings to community members and other educational researchers. While some may term their presentations as *testimonios* (Huber, 2010), counter-stories (Solorzano and Yosso, 2002), and auto-ethnographies (Camangian, 2010), we also infer that the students' presentations of their research findings are exemplars of critical pedagogy. In this paper, we document the ways in which CYR students create innovative ways to capture the attentions of their audience and engage them in a learning process about their research.

We analyze students' presentations and their pedagogical approaches to challenge traditional notions of educational research by questioning the relevancy and applicability of purely adult-driven educational research. The students' pedagogy and voices are driven by their existential experiences in under-resourced, inequitable schooling systems. Therefore, in evaluating learning conditions in urban public schools and reforming educational structures, this paper concludes that the legitimization and consideration of youth research contributes significantly to educational research, organizing, and reform.

Pedagogy of Digital Media: Transformative Uses of Technology in the Council of Youth Research

Participatory media tools like digital social networks and websites like YouTube have fundamentally changed the culture of learning in which young people are immersed (Thomas and Brown, 2011). Further, while there are myriad opportunities to engage in new media learning practices, researchers have identified a "participation gap" that divides meaningful engagement with new media tools by race and class in ways that mirrors the U.S. academic achievement gap (Jenkins, 2008; Margolis, 2008). Although urban youth are gaining increased access to participatory digital technology, they lack access to education that fosters the kinds of sophisticated skills in computer programming that can help them become producers of digital content, rather than simply consumers (Kellner & Share, 2009). At the same time, urban youth too often are not offered meaningful opportunities to formally engage in political and civic life and analyze the conditions that they experience on a daily basis. Reform efforts in schools and other social institutions largely fail to honor the voices of young people and engage them in decision making about issues that affect their lives; adults make decisions for young people rather than with them. While there is burgeoning research around the role that participatory media plays to improve learning, few models exist that engage urban youth in the creation of such media or do so with the goal of increasing civic engagement.

In this paper, the students, teachers, and university researchers of the Council of Youth Research examine the role of new media in developing young people into critical civic agents. We seek to understand how young people use participatory media spaces for the purposes of collective political and civic engagement while gaining the skills needed to succeed in the information economy. We will analyze the online presence of the Council and explains how students utilize new media tools such as YouTube, Facebook, blogs, and Twitter.

We will explore how students in the Council seek to mobilize others through extending their learning well beyond existing digital media models aimed at youth. Instead of hacking, programming, and engaging in alternative computing practices for the sake of mere computational literacies, we present data in this paper that shows the use of digital media tools for transformative civic purposes. Developing technological literacy in the Council of Youth Research strives to arm a generation of urban youth with the intellectual and social capital to leverage change within a large and diverse population while simultaneously preparing them for the information economy.

This paper also analyzes the digital videos that have been produced by Council students and disseminated on YouTube as tools that foster increased academic and civic participation for youth. We explore how urban youth act as producers and consumers of critical digital media. As we anticipate more youth utilizing these applications and new media products, this work will help us to think about how to educate and organize a more technologically savvy and able citizenry ready for democratic participation in 2011 and beyond.

Re-Defining Civic Engagement: Using Research to Transform Democracy in the Council of Youth Research

A growing consensus in the field of civic education is that civics should not be about teaching "techniques" or "routines" or delivering "programs" of civic knowledge, but should be considered a continuous practice through which citizens become co-creators of their own social and political environments (Cammarota & Fine, 2008; Morrell, 2004). In this paper, the students, teachers, and university researchers of the Council of Youth Research will examine how the Council is striving to generate grounded theory about civic learning that challenges the commonly held view that low-income and minority students are "deficient" in civic skills and engagement (Levinson, 2007). We will show how citizenship is taught in the community through offering students opportunities to engage in meaningful and authentic processes in a critical community of practice.

The work of the Council is based on the idea that students learn civic knowledge, skills and dispositions best when they are embedded within practices that relate to their developing identities and daily lived experiences—an idea that emerges from established theories of learning. Vygotsky (1978) focuses on the role of culture and social interactions in the construction of knowledge, and Lave and Wenger (1991) argue that learning is socially constructed, as students take peripheral and then more central roles in "communities of practice" that scaffold actions and behaviors. Each of these perspectives highlights the need for learning to be active, grounded in social interaction, and guided by practice. These criteria match up well with practice-oriented theories of citizenship, which stress that citizenship is continually negotiated in everyday social situations rather than a static body of knowledge or skills that can be simply acquired (Lawy & Biesta, 2007; Nasir & Kirshner, 2003). As Lawy and Biesta note, "young people learn to be citizens as a consequence of their participation in the actual practices that make up their lives" (p. 45).

This paper explores how youth within the Council of Youth Research reshape our understanding of democracy in multiple ways. Namely, it looks at the process of youth participation in a democratic public and the role of learning through written and oral presentations the students produce. This study finds that these efforts concretize the role of youth, who become more legitimate democratic participants. Through a combination of standpoint theory and case study analysis, our analysis of the Council reveals pedagogical and curricular strategies that encourage citizenship-as-practice and can be broadly applied across contexts both in classrooms and in extracurricular spaces to empower urban youth to transformative civic agency.

Using a grounded theory approach to analyzing student interviews, presentations, videos and reflections, this paper offers an in-depth discussion of how the student work is reflective of the process of becoming part of the public. This study highlights the connection between this transformative process and larger democratic themes of equity, access, and participation. The results point toward ways that the Council of Youth Research strives to embody a Deweyan notion of the public which challenges the passive, adult-centered views of young people that characterizes many civic engagement efforts.

Reconceptualizing Communities of Practice: Literacy, Learning, and Identity Development in the Council of Youth Research

In this paper, the students, teachers, and university researchers in the Council explore how the framework of communities of practice (Lave and Wenger, 1991) can be reformulated by looking at literacy, learning, and identity development within the Council and community organizing groups. To investigate how the Council illuminates the concept of communities of practice, we sought to address the following research question: How can the literacy, learning, and identity development processes in the Council help flesh out the concept of communities of practice? To answer these questions, we conducted participant observations and interviews, and collected student work products. We then analyzed the data through critical discourse analysis and ethnographic data reduction. We find that the Council not only exemplifies the concept of a community of practice, but also expands this concept through its application to youth organizing contexts.

Lave & Wenger (1991) define a community of practice as "a set of relations among persons, activity, and world, over time and in relation with other tangential and overlapping communities of practice" (p. 98). To account for the situated character of learning in communities of practice, they propose the concept of "legitimate peripheral participation" to describe the ways that individuals occupy certain positions and have certain amounts of power. Learning or development within a community of practice involves members' changing participation in activities over time, moving toward full participation (Lave & Wenger, 1991; Rogoff, 2003).

We find in this paper that the Council exemplifies a close-knit community of practice that helps students construct empowered identities oriented toward action through the authentic learning associated with community action. Additionally, Council students inhabit various and shifting identities that develop along with their literacy learning, demonstrating that communities of practice can be much more dynamic than Lave and Wenger postulated.

This paper finds that within the Council's community of practice, students engage in a range of both critical and academic literacy practices, including: video documentary production and distribution; the use of social networking sites to promote events and spread information; conducting videotaped interviews with stakeholders; and giving presentations. However, beyond Lave and Wenger's description of learning in a community of practice, students' change in participation within the Council occurs in a highly dynamic fashion. Students (both novices to the program and those who are more experienced) participate in literacy activities in multiple and shifting ways over time and at any given moment.

Our paper explores how identity development is not a simple progression from periphery to center as learning occurs within the Council. Students must inhabit a range of spaces whereby their status can differ dramatically. At one moment they may be presenting at a national conference, and at the next they may be students of a teacher who devalues them. This paper finds that, over time, students gain identities as researchers and change agents who do not only consume media but produce it as well.

References

Camangian, P. (2010). Starting with self: Teaching autoethnography to foster critically caring literacies. *Research in the Teaching of English, 45*(2), 179–204.

Cammarota, J., & Fine, M. (Eds.). (2008). *Revolutionizing education: Youth participatory action research in motion.* New York: Routledge.

Dewey, J. (1932/1990). *The child and the curriculum/The school and society.* Chicago: University of Chicago Press.

Duncan-Andrade, J., and Morrell, E. (2008). *The art of critical pedagogy: Possibilities for moving from theory to practice in urban schools.* New York: Peter Lang.

Freire, P. (1970) *Pedagogy of the oppressed.* New York: Continuum.

Ginwright, S., & James, T. (2002). From assets to agents of change: Social justice, organizing, and youth development. *New directions for youth development, 96,* 27–46.

Huber, L. (2010). Disrupting apartheid of knowledge: Testimonio as methodology in Latina/o critical race research in education. *International Journal of Qualitative Studies in Education, 654*(16), 639–654.

Jenkins, H. (2008). *Convergence culture: Where old and new media collide.* New York: New York University Press.

Kellner, D., & Share, J. (2009). Critical media education and radical democracy. In *The Routledge International Handbook of Critical Education* (pp. 281–295). M. W. Apple, W. Au, and L. A. Gandin (Eds.). New York: Routledge.

Lave, J., and Wenger, E. (1991). *Situated learning: Legitimate peripheral participation.* Cambridge: Cambridge University Press.

Lawy, R., & Biesta, G. (2007). Citizenship-as-practice: The educational implications of an inclusive and relational understanding of citizenship. *British Journal of Educational Studies, 54*(1), 34–50.

Lee, C. D. (2007). *Culture, literacy, & learning: taking bloom in the midst of the whirlwind.* New York, NY: Teachers College Press.

Levinson, M. (2007). The civic achievement gap. CIRCLE Working Paper 51, College Park, MD.

Margolis, J. (2008). *Stuck in the shallow end: Education, race, and computing.* Cambridge, MA: MIT Press.

McIntyre, A. (2000). Constructing meaning about violence, school, and community: Participatory action research with urban youth. *Urban Review, 32*(2), 123–154.

Mediratta, K., Shah, S., & McAlister, S. (2009). *Community organizing for stronger schools: Strategies and successes.* Cambridge: Harvard Educational Press.

Morrell, E. (2004). *Becoming critical researchers: Literacy and empowerment for urban youth.* New York: Peter Lang.

Nasir, N., & Kirshner, B. (2003). The cultural construction of moral and civic identities. *Applied Developmental Science, 7,* 138–147.

Rogoff, B. (2003). *The cultural nature of human development.* Oxford: Oxford University Press.

Solorzano, D., & Yosso, T. (2002). Critical race methodology: Counterstorytelling as an analytical framework for education research. *Qualitative Inquiry, 8*(1), 23–44.

Thomas, D., & Brown, J. S. (2011). *A new culture of learning: Cultivating the imagination for a world of constant change.* CreateSpace.

Valenzuela, A. (1999). *Subtractive schooling: U.S.–Mexican youth and the politics of caring.* Albany: SUNY Press.

Vygotsky, L. (1978). *Mind in society.* Cambridge: Harvard University Press.

APPENDIX E

Scholarly Publications Authored by Adult Members of the Council about YPAR

Bautista, M., Bertrand, M., Morrell, E., Scorza, D., & Matthews, C. (2013). Participatory Action Research and city youth: Methodological insights from the Council of Youth Research. *Teachers College Record, 115*(10), 1–23.

Bertrand, M. (2014). Reciprocal dialogue between educational decision-makers and students of color: Opportunities and obstacles. *Educational Administration Quarterly, 50*(5), 812–843.

Duncan-Andrade, J., & Morrell, E. (2008). *The art of critical pedagogy: Possibilities for moving from theory to practice in urban schools.* New York: Peter Lang.

Garcia, A., Mirra, N., Morrell, E., Martinez, A., & Scorza, D. (2015). The Council of Youth Research: Critical literacy and civic agency in the digital age. *Reading & Writing Quarterly (31)*2, 151–167.

Mirra, N., & Morrell, E. (2011). Teachers as civic agents: Toward a critical democratic theory of urban teacher development. *Journal of Teacher Education, 62*(4), 408–420.

Mirra, N., Morrell, E., Cain, E., Scorza, D., & Ford, A. (2013). Educating for a critical democracy: Civic participation re-imagined in the Council of Youth Research. *Democracy and Education 21*(1), Article 3.

Morrell, E. (2008). *Critical literacy and urban youth: Pedagogies of access, dissent, and liberation.* New York: Routledge.

Rogers, J., & Morrell, E. (2006). Becoming critical public historians: Students study diversity and access in post "Brown v. Board" Los Angeles. *Social Education, 70*(6), 366–369.

Scorza, D., Mirra, N., & Morrell, E. (2013). It should just be education: Critical pedagogy normalized as academic excellence. *International Journal of Critical Pedagogy 4*(2), 15–34.

INDEX